I0155638

FIND YOUR VOICE

Your Superpower & Passion Unleashed

For communications, public speaking,
broadcasting, podcasting, and life

Michelle M. Mendoza

FIND YOUR VOICE
Your Superpower & Passion Unleashed

Copyright © 2022 by Michelle M. Mendoza

Published by

Bitterroot Mountain Publishing House LLC
P.O. Box 3508, Hayden, ID 83835
Visit our website at www.BMPHmedia.com

Interior and Cover design by Jera Publishing

All rights reserved. No part of this book may be used or reproduced by any means, graphic, electronic, or mechanical, including photocopying, recording, taping or by any information storage retrieval system without the written permission of the author except in the case of brief quotations embodied in critical articles and reviews.

For questions or information regarding permission for excerpts please contact Bitterroot Mountain Publishing House at Editor@BMPHmedia.com.

ISBN: 978-1-940025-69-8 (paperback)
ISBN: 978-1-940025-70-4 (eBook)

Library of Congress Control Number: 2022923501

ACKNOWLEDGMENTS

To every one of you who are in my world as family, friends, interviews, colleagues, you impact my life. Your presence enhances my world, and you are greatly appreciated. You are a part of sharing my own voice.

To Joshua, my tech support and continual joy since the day of your birth.

To Giselle, my delight and my dearest friend.

To John Jr. and. John Sr., for your care and for helping me to understand superpowers.

The treasure I possess in my friends who got me on track, encouraged and supported me in this venture, I thank you as well. To Darol. To Gail & John, Aunt Meri, Glo, Bob, my family.

To Carl, for your never-ending support and love.

And in memory of you, mom, Mary Mendoza, your sacrifice, and legacy live on in those you invested your voice so greatly in.

Finally, all glory to my precious Lord who knows the plans He has for me and to whom my voice will sing. LOVE YOU ALL!

CONTENTS

INTRODUCTION

YOUR VOICE IS important and there is an audience out there, waiting to hear it.

Never before has access to individual expression been as attainable. Never before has it been as easy to speak, teach, podcast, broadcast, make videos, create blogs, or author books. My intent is to help you find that precious passion within you, fine tune it into a powerful message, develop *superpowers* that can carry it out, and build a strategy for presenting that message to the world. Do you believe that it is time to cultivate your passion? I do! Your voice was made for such a time as this.

> *Nine hundred years of time and space and I've never met someone who wasn't important.*
> — The Doctor

Within this quote is the skeleton key to finding and expressing your voice. It comes from the longest running science fiction series in television history, *Doctor Who.* The show first aired in 1963 and is still a favorite today.

To give perspective to the quote, the Doctor is a Time Lord from the planet Gallifrey. He has two hearts and an extraordinary regenerative attribute that contributes to his longevity.

Traveling through space and time for hundreds of years in his time machine, the TARDIS, he has encounters on far-flung planets, dodged dangers at the end of time itself, and traveled beyond imaginative extraterrestrial worlds through our earthly history. This character watched the fires of Mount Vesuvius as they erupted over the unsuspecting city of Pompei. He witnessed the inner torment and brilliance of Vincent Van Gogh firsthand. From Cleopatra to Winston Churchill, this fictional personality wove his way through the very best of mankind. Yet, in his vast and unimaginable journeys, he concluded that every person is important.

What a powerful line to have written into the script of a sci-fi television series. Every single person has value. Every voice is important.

My voice has been broadcast over the airwaves to millions of people. I forged my experience on local music radio stations, syndicated talk shows, international programs on multiple continents, television, and the big screen. Now my voice is podcasted, broadcasted, and vodcasted via the internet. Conducting thousands of interviews with movers, shakers, and heads of state is thought to be a feather in the ol' cap of a broadcaster. The truth is that the everyday person has just as much to say and to learn from as any big-name celebrity. In all my years of experience, I have never met anyone who was not important.

How does that relate to finding and expressing your voice? You are important! Your voice is important! Like the discovery of the individuality of every sparkling snowflake, you glisten in your own unique way and can catch the attention of a potential audience. That importance is the essence of finding and sharing your voice. Your passion and its expression are crucial. There is an audience waiting to hear what you have to say. No one else can fill your role like you can.

The people of the world are important and have value and you and your important voice will enhance their important lives. It is a beautiful, symbiotic ballet of edification and pedagogy. In all the world's history, in all the known universe, there is not now, there never has been, and there will never be another you. This is your time in history to share your voice.

What is it about your voice that makes it so important to find? It is the focusing and sharing of your passion, your knowledge, and your unique life experiences. Since you drew your first breath as a wet bundle of newborn joy, squealing your first shriek to the world, everything you have done, accomplished, failed at, cherished, loathed, learned, loved, and experienced has become part of your story. Think of it as the hard drive of your soul. It has been filling with data your entire lifetime and holds boundless files of life lessons, stories, and know-how that someone out there is hungering for. All that delicious information sits like an email message on your human computer. The world is waiting for you to hit send.

It sounds easy enough. Though, with nearly eight billion human souls populating our planet, if human expression were as easy as the press of a send button, the entire earth would be a rich cacophony of passions and voices. It is not. Everyone would be doing it. They are not. Many live a lifetime of quiet disappointment, having never felt as though they have been truly heard. If we could learn how to cultivate our own voice, how to express it, and where to share it, the world would be richer for it.

Competition for your voice can be fierce. As of this writing, there are over two-million podcasts comprising over forty-eight million episodes. YouTube has one billion videos watched per day. Each year, there are nearly a million books published in the United States alone. Firing up your computer, recording content, and hitting send will not guarantee that anyone will care.

What if someone who has walked this path before shared her life lessons with you? What if she could help you cultivate your voice, format your message, and share that message to the world? What if she could show you the tools, instructions, and equipment that she uses to produce, publish, and market her voice? In sharing these treasures with you, you, in turn, can use them to find, build, and keep audiences enthralled. By reading and internalizing the lessons I've learned, my hope is that your life will be enhanced and you will be well on your way to sharing your voice, reaching people, and enhancing their lives. My hope is that this cycle of edification, engagement, and enlightenment will continue with this book being an investment in your life so that you, in turn, may invest in the lives of others.

There are a host of changes in our society that have created a need for specific voices like yours. Changes in the media and changes in social behaviors have generated new openings for expression. Developments in technology and how we interact with it has impacted how we communicate. Any new voice will need to navigate an ever-changing labyrinth of voices.

Radio broadcasting, in the years before television, had an extraordinarily powerful reach. In days past, it looked much different than today, with variety shows, dramas, and live performances. Radio was a serious business and broadcasters were the cream of the crop of communicators in their time. Television invaded our lives and the old radio technology had to transform with the times to survive.

Another hit to radio came in 1981 as a new venue exploded on television. Just after midnight on August 1, MTV, a.k.a. Music Television, began to televise its new format of continuous music videos. The video chosen to break into the world of broadcasting was, "Video Killed the Radio Star" by The Buggles. The song spoke its message loud and clear and I remember watching, wide-eyed that night, as history was made. Traditional radio was proclaimed dead. Video had seemingly killed the radio star.

Radio adapted, once again, as music radio promoted videos and, in turn, videos promoted music in a cooperative dance. Talk radio boomed in this era as well, with new, politically alternative voices. Radio had embraced the changing times and powered through.

In 1992, the MTV network started backing away from music videos. By the early 2020s, no music videos could be found on the network. The internet and ease of downloads killed the video star. Radio struggled but lived on.

New challenges to radio have entered the stage today. There has been an onslaught of satellite and internet radio stations. Podcasts, vodcasts, and music on demand have stolen our attention. Up and down the dial, local radio stations are struggling to stay alive. Stations, trying to save costs, have homogenized. Radio outlets are in effect turning into an audio McDonald's where you can order the same thing at any location and it all tastes the same. Revenue for radio advertising has been declining yearly since 2015. In 2018, the 850-station strong radio conglomerate iHeartMedia filed for bankruptcy. The competition and inability to change fostered a need for new and unique ideas.

Nothing lasts forever but changes create opportunity. We can either embrace the change or go down with the ship. Radio stations that limp along could take advantage of the loss of personal touch that conglomerates and satellite have created. If they change with the needs of the times, they will endure the times. Change leaves room for others to start something entirely new.

New ideas flourish online. Today, there are endless ways to share your voice, utilizing the most modern technologies. Think about it. Anyone can broadcast with the technology that you hold right in your hand, a smartphone. These changes have created a shift. They have made the menu of information explode. They have opened the previously exclusive door of broadcasting to everyone.

Additionally, the current state of news media has generated a need for new voices. No matter your political leanings, we have all experienced the frustration with media that focuses on entertainment, exploitation, spin doctoring, and unbalanced, unverified reporting. Celebrity news, who is hooking up with whom, and the culture of demonization have all become part of the daily news cycle. Media will sometimes deliver only part of the story, leaving vital information on the cutting room floor. Newsrooms will gather information from press releases and report it as fact, without research. Unconfirmed information is doled out and picked up by other outlets in a rush to grab the audience's attention. The changes leave a craving in the public's stomach for the rest of the story.

I remember when changes in the media world crept into my work in the newsroom. When I was a young radio and television news writer, it was a badge of honor to write politically divisive or emotionally charged news stories in such a way that the reader, listener, or viewer had no idea what my particular leanings were. It was about researching and reporting without bias and with integrity. At my writer's desk during an election cycle, I typed out a story about a presidential candidate who was making his way to our city. My editor held the printed story in his hands, glasses halfway down his nose, evaluating my piece. I detected a satisfying air of approval on his face. My pride turned ice cold when he lowered the page and schooled me in the art of consumer manipulation. He told me that my piece was good. However, if I were to word things just right, we could make people think more favorably about the candidate. The ends, he said, would justify the means. Why leave people to think for themselves? "We are in a position of power and should use our power to move the masses in the right direction," he said.

The news has messed with our minds, and we know it. In 2021, Gallup released a new poll tracking the public's confidence in a variety of key institutions. Where the media was concerned, more than three-quarters of the public did not have much confidence in newspapers or television.[1] The numbers in

---

[1] Megan Brenan. "Americans' Confidence in Major U.S. Institutions Dips." Gallup, July 14, 2021. https://news.gallup.com/poll/352316/americans-confidence-major-institutions-dips.

similar polls are astounding, reaching across political leanings and affiliations. Additionally, the algorithms of social media feed us only what we want to hear.

Research published in 2009 in a journal of the American Psychological Association analyzed data from ninety-one studies and nearly eight-thousand participants. It found that people were generally twice as likely to choose information that supported their own point of view than to consider opposing ideas.[2] It is as though we crave the propaganda that has become so integrated into our daily lives. Somewhere along the line, the light comes on and we find ourselves in need of something more. The American media have a problem as the light comes on for many. The art of consumer manipulation and control leaves people desiring a new voice.

Then there is *cancel culture.* This phenomenon generates a void waiting to be filled by new voices. Cancel culture is a phrase rising out of a twenty-first century trend of canceling, withdrawing support, disallowing, firing, de-platforming, or shouting down those with whom we disagree. Despite good intentions and the idea that it is simply holding others accountable, the consequences of shutting down other ideas in lieu of honest debate leads to stagnation and a need for new ideas to enter the conversation.

The phrase *settled science* contributes to the canceling of alternative ideas and discoveries. Science, however, by definition, must be poked and prodded, challenged and evaluated. It is never settled. New discoveries must be allowed to confront widely accepted beliefs. Then our beliefs can be better understood and empowered. In other cases, it can be dismantled in pursuit of better understanding. There is an intrinsic human need for challenge and discovery. In shutting out new or disfavored ideas, we create a desire for voices to break through barriers to fill the silence. That voice could be yours.

Yet another idiosyncrasy of our time that is opening doors for new voices is unbridled access to information. It has made people thirsty for more. Whatever you can imagine that ignites interest within you, you can find someone talking about it. There is likely a page, shared video, program, or teaching out there already discussing the topic. All of this is available at the touch of your fingers.

---

[2] Albarracín W. Hart, "Feeling validated versus being correct: A meta-analysis of selective exposure to information." *Psychological Bulletin*, 135 no. 4, (2009): 555-588.

In the days before internet access, information was not as easy to find. A visit to the library was your best bet at researching ideas, hobbies, and interests. You could hire an expert or travel somewhere to take classes. All these outlets required time and effort. Today, the information of the world's libraries, the expertise of masters, and enlightenment from classes on just about anything are more accessible and affordable than at any time in history, all thanks to technology. With more than 4.5 billion people active on the internet worldwide, a good 59.5 percent of the global population, and over 80 percent of adults in the United States accessing online information daily[3], there is an audience somewhere among them hungry for what you have to share.

The fifth century BC Chinese writer, philosopher, and military strategist Sun Tzu said, "In the midst of chaos, there is also opportunity."[4] The selective exclusion of facts, the loss of objectivity in the media, the shutting down of opinions, the onslaught of information all leave a thirst for new voices. Ease of access to information and the chaos of so many voices require you to focus your message to reach your specific audience.

Each section and chapter of this book is framed to laser focus your voice to reach the ever-growing number of people that need it most. It is designed to keep you from getting lost in the cacophony of other voices. It is meant to give you an understanding of how to find and best engage your audience. You will get help in recognizing your communication superpower for creating, focusing, formatting, sharing, and celebrating your voice.

Additionally, I have created a separate devotional for those who would like to dig deeper. Finding spiritual roots and grounding your worldview gives you a more effective base to share your voice from. This devotional is complimentary and can be found at www.findyourvoice.fun.

Every person is important and every important person has a passion. Every passion craves a voice for expression, every voice needs a platform, and every platform needs an audience. Helping you to find your voice and focus it to reach and keep a waiting audience and enhance the world is my passion and purpose for this book.

---

[3] Statista, "United States: digital population 2021," Accessed September 7, 2021 https://www.statista.com/statistics/1044012/usa-digital-platform-audience.
[4] Sun Tzu, *Art of War* (Engage Classic, 2020)

FIND YOUR VOICE SECTIONS

*F*IND YOUR VOICE is written in five sections. Each section gives you a different bent on finding and expressing your voice. Some sections may be more in line with your perceived needs than others. All the sections and chapters can maximize the understanding of your message, help extract your epiphany and passion, and empower your delivery. You will also learn what tools professionals have developed and how to use them to relate to and grow your audience.

SECTION 1: CULTIVATE YOUR VOICE

When you are grounded from your core, you can more powerfully reach out from that core to others. This section will take you through fears and failures and doubts and disappointments to spark the passion that will make you powerful and relevant.

SECTION 2: NICHE YOUR VOICE

When you learn to focus your voice, you discover how to spotlight your passions and communicate them to others. Learn how to make your message clear and concise. Identify your audience and consolidate your epiphanies and experiences into your niche.

SECTION 3: SUPERPOWER YOUR VOICE

Learn what four superpowers every communication effort needs to succeed. Identify your communications strengths. Learn how to use these superpowers to translate your message and passions to the world. Recognize your *Kryptonite*, your weaknesses, and how to overcome them.

SECTION 4: PLATFORM YOUR VOICE

Discover the ideal platform for your message. Build and equip the right setting for your passion to magnify your voice. Tailor your message for your chosen outlet. Prepare to share your voice with the world.

SECTION 5: CELEBRATE YOUR VOICE

How do you keep your passion fresh? Learn how to feed your soul so that you can use your new outlet to inspire your passion in others and impact the world.

SECTION 1

CULTIVATE YOUR VOICE

It took me quite a long time to develop a voice, and now that I have it, I am not going to be silent.

—Madeleine Korbel Albright,
first woman to be U.S. Secretary of State

SECTION 4

CULTIVATE YOUR VOICE

CHAPTER 1:

MAGNUM OPUS

Your Voice as Superpower Masterpiece

LIVE MUSIC AND catered food delighted the crowd of partygoers at a large summertime gathering being hosted at a waterfront restaurant in Seattle. As with any party, people mingled, laughed, and chatted about the news of the day. A small group gathered on a wooden deck overlooking the dark waters of Elliott Bay. The music and scent of the sea permeated through the twilight.

I cannot recall the topic, but as I conversed with a small group, I remember voicing an opinion, adding to the mix. Mid-sentence, something astonishing happened. Imagine speaking to a group and suddenly it is as though your words become enchanted. They ring out like a siren's song beckoning anyone within earshot to hang upon every sentence. The crowd grew, and I was both invigorated and intimidated. Their eyes were wide and mouths agape. I was amazed. Then I realized that it was not me who they were fascinated with. Standing directly behind me was a very well-known local radio talk show host and political figure. The crowd did not hear a word I had said, they were simply star-struck at the figure over my shoulder.

Do you know who was listening to me? That local celebrity. While the crowds looked past, he was intent on my words and demeanor. He remarked, "You're a little firecracker. Have you ever considered talk radio?" He invited me to guest host his radio talk show and from there, my long and successful career was launched.

You are like a piece of art. There is someone out there ready to glean from the masterpiece that you are. Some might look past you, like those walking past the works of Monet to view the Picasso. They may find themselves mesmerized and deeply touched by the Rembrandts featured prominently in the gallery display. Your voice will not captivate everyone, nor will mine. For those to whom you are meant to speak, however, your voice will impact their world. I could never be that talk show host at the party who captivated the crowd. I do not have his talent, experience, education, or passion. I do not, however, need to be him. The world already has one of him. I can and should be my own unique work of art. I need only to be me. Am I special? Absolutely, as are you!

In my view, we are all created in a magnificent form, images of God. We have this common inheritance. Realization of this heritage can empower you to fill an exclusive roll that was meant for you alone. Find that roll, that passion, and you have tapped into your unique voice.

Every one of us has magnificent distinctiveness in our unique voice. Some are boisterous and exciting, some soft and thought provoking. Your voice is your own. It need not be like anyone else's. No one can truly replace you and your calling, which has been cultivated and effectively expressed in your life story.

Why is it that many people live an entire lifetime never having found their voice? There are countless factors that swoop in and stunt our expressions before they are successfully heard. You may lack understanding in how to unlock your voice. Naivety in communication can bring us to failure. Fear or past failure is often the root of our impediments.

One secret to breakthrough is the realization that our greatest strengths are found in weakness. Even many communication professionals fail to realize that fear and failure can actually be our allies. Weakness helps us to relate to others and truly makes us relatable in return. Imperfections can strengthen our ability to empathically communicate our message. It is our perceived failings and our humanity that are our secret weapons.

Think back to one of your most embarrassing moments, your worst attempt at expression. Do you remember the burning in your chest? A fire of shame rose up your neck, beading sweat formed on your brow. You ignited with the reddening of your face. *Psychology Today* explains the actual need we have as humans and as a society for embarrassment. "Most researchers believe that the purpose of embarrassment is to make people feel badly about their social or personal mistakes as a form of internal (or societal) feedback so that they learn not to repeat the error. The accompanying physiological changes, including blushing, sweating, or stammering, may signal to others that a person recognizes their own error, and so is not cold-hearted or oblivious."[5] If we are willing to embrace growth, shame and embarrassment can be learning tools and a sign that we too are humans seeking betterment. Others see us in our vulnerability. They commiserate and respect us. They are then much more willing to listen.

Conversely, we can run from fear and failure. If we do, we miss out on the growth that is birthed through difficulty. Without these life lessons, we may never achieve a higher plane of humanhood and relatability.

While I have never craved being the center of attention, I do love doing the things that seem to put me there. Music, acting, public speaking, dance; there are few ways to enjoy these gifts that do not eventually lead to the spotlight. While my life had me on a fast track to center stage, fear, insecurity, and failure could have shut me down before I ever had the chance to shine.

We are each endowed with our own raw talent. Training can feed the volume of our talent, but there are many things that can mute it. There will always be something that threatens to extinguish our light. Perhaps there is a time that you keep hidden in the recesses of your mind. You may have locked away the memory of pain, failure, fear, or intimidation that effectively held you back.

Even the greats have their stories of failure. One of humanity's greatest artists was Michelangelo. Fraud and failure could have destroyed his rise to prominence and timeless appreciation, though. "In 1496, Michelangelo made a sleeping cupid figure and treated it with acidic earth to make it seem ancient. He then sold it to a dealer, Baldassare del Milanese, who in turn sold it to Cardinal Romario of San Giorgio. Romario heard rumors of the scam demanding his money back. He was quite impressed by Michelangelo's skill and invited him to Rome for a meeting. The young sculptor would linger in

---

[5] Psychology Today, "Embarrassment," Accessed October 19, 2021, https://www. psychologytoday.com/us/basics/embarrassment.

the Eternal City for the next several years, eventually winning a commission to carve *The Pieta*, the work that first made his name as an artist."[6] Michelangelo had to fight subsequent accusations of fraud and doubt. He spent many a year building his reputation and overcoming that failure of his youth as he grew his talent and esteem. Some have said that his struggle magnified his understanding and need of redemption, which became so evident in his work.

I am no Michelangelo, but at the early age of ten, I wanted to be a virtuoso, nickel-plated flute in hand. Seeking to cultivate my musical talent, my parents enrolled me in classes. Part of the American experience for middle-class kids in our society is lessons, classes, and coaching. These rights of passage all seem to culminate in a mandatory, must-show-your-parents-what-they-are-paying-for event. For me, it was a recital.

I was paired with a fellow student in my age group for a duet. When the time came, we were practiced and prepared for our piece. We stood before the sullen crowd seated in metal chairs, surrounded by racks of music books and instruments that were hung for sale. The only thing separating our duo from the small gathering of serious-faced parents and students was a standard, black metal music stand. That just did not seem enough to protect us.

Looking up at an audience, the body can be overtaken with that familiar quiver of nerves that manifests in humiliating displays of awkwardness. As we began our piece, my partner yielded to a sudden attack of the *death giggle*. Nervous laughter paralyzed her performance. I could not continue as the infectious laughter, in turn, overtook me. No matter how I tried, I could not form an embouchure as my mouth involuntarily stretched into a nervous chuckle.

They might as well have used a gong and a shepherd's hook to yank us off the makeshift stage, in shame. The embarrassment was momentary, but my parents' disappointment etched that day in my memory. What if, at the age of ten, I never took to the stage again? My life would be drastically different. The joy I have from my career never would have been realized. Rather, I had to learn from that moment and find a way to never let that kind of embarrassment overtake me again.

---

6   Michelangelo.org. "10 Interesting Facts You Might Not Know about Michelangelo," Accessed October 21, 2021, https://www.michelangelo.org/michelangelo-facts.jsp.

Your voice is a unique song. It is accompanied by the music of your life. In fact, your life is a bit of a symphonic masterpiece comprised of your own talent, experiences, and passions. Even failures and moments of shame factor into the piece that is your ballad.

Magnum opus is Latin for an important work of art. It is considered the most important work of an artist's life. It is a masterwork. The intricacy and grandeur that make up who you are defies words. You are, in all your victories and failures, without a doubt, a masterpiece.

Think of just the physical marvels that are at work in you. Your body hosts an amalgamation of different systems that function in unison, like the instruments in an orchestra working together to form a single symphony. You have, at this very moment, billions of chemical interactions and a circulation system that is a wonder of engineering. Your brain is a sentient computer with neurons zooming around at roughly 120 kilometers per second. That is just a part of your physical make up. The soul factor is equally miraculous. You are "fearfully and wonderfully made" (Ps 139:14), a magnum opus.

Your success, your masterpiece revealed, relies on finding your voice and getting that work of art that is you, presented before the world. Can you imagine if the works of the world's master artists never made their way to museums and galleries for our viewing? Vincent Van Gogh's *A Starry Night* would not be found today on living room walls, handbags, coffee mugs, tube socks, nor embossed on my favorite travel guitar. Van Gogh's voice-through-art was hushed during his living years only to be celebrated after his death. Now, long after his departing in 1890, Van Gogh's voice is vibrant. His art was his soul's voice. What is yours? How glorious it will be to paint the world with your voice in your lifetime and perhaps beyond!

A voice can become more than someone ever imagined it could be. A 1995 movie directed by Stephen Herek and starring Richard Dreyfuss tells the story of a high school music teacher who dreams of composing his own masterpiece. He believes there is one piece of music that will be his defining moment in history. As family and life sweep by with the passage of time, along with them go his dream and music. His piece goes unpublished and unplayed. Upon his retirement, the students who his talent had touched gathered in the school auditorium. To a standing ovation, they pay homage to his investment in them. Picking up their instruments, three decades of past music class pupils perform his symphony, his masterpiece. They, his students, and his family, are the stunning success of his life. The movie is called *Mr. Holland's Opus.*

The world is full of masterpieces. Every museum holds collections of fine art. The world is all the better each time one hangs, framed in completion. As you ponder that thought, remember that you too are a work of art portrayed in your life's passions. With each fine painting, it is not just the main subject, but many other factors of color, lighting, brush strokes, and background that make a completed piece. It is not only the grand accomplishments of your life that are worth celebrating, but also the struggles, the trials, the tears, and the beautiful works that touch others in simple but profound ways and complete your stunning portrayal.

Communication will help frame and display you in your grandeur. The word communication is derived from two Latin words. *Communis* means common, as in having something in common. It is the same root for the word communal. *Communicare* means to share. Together they form the idea that you possess something that you want others to partake of. You must engage in the act and art of effective sharing or communication to make that thing common to both you and the recipient.

Somewhere along the line, you have developed a passion which you would like others to feast upon. You have ideas, talents, and experiences to share. You may need to sell yourself for a job. You might have to close a sale, give a presentation, or engage in an on-air interview to share your story. There may be dreams of writing a blog or book. You may just want to effectively be heard. You can find your own unique voice, develop your masterpiece and, as we work together, learn the art of communication for sharing the magnum opus that is you.

CHAPTER 2:

PILLARS OF IMPERFECTION

Imperfections superpower your voice

PERCHED MAJESTICALLY ATOP a limestone hill, some five-hundred feet above the Ilissos Valley in Athens, Greece, the Parthenon stands in ancient glory. The nearly 2,500-year-old marvel of architecture, art, and engineering has an iconic stature and is visited by about 7.2 million people each year. Though not in its original grandeur, the Parthenon, with its massive and distinctive ribbed Doric columns, is still a stunning sight to behold today. There is a mysterious power in the design of the Parthenon that can be a lesson for us today.

Think of all you have weathered in your lifetime. You've got nothing on the Parthenon. The passage of time on the temple had a dynamic effect. The structure suffered from neglect, vandalism, occupation, earthquakes, and explosions that chipped away its acclaim. One of the structure's most devastating blows came in 1687. While being used as an Ottoman ammunition dump site, the ammunition was ignited by a Venetian bombardment. Explosions caused substantial damage to the structure and the stunning statuaries within. Battered, bruised, and broken, it still stands as a recognizable wonder. The Parthenon is a testament to endurance, splendor, and engineering.

Some of the same principles that have upheld this spectacle of antiquity can help you build a foundation from which your soul can thrive and your voice can find expression. What secrets does the Parthenon hold? You may be surprised.

The Parthenon was created with purposeful imperfections. Flaws were engineered into its design by the architects and sculptors who created it. Though the structure has a beautifully symmetrical appearance, it is in fact, not straight. It is gently curved from the foundation to its roof. The block steps leading up the front are slightly tilted. Columns are angled inward, and the corner pillars possess more girth than the others. All of the columns are formed thicker, swollen in the middle sections. The front of the structure is slightly higher on the West side, sloping towards the East. These subtle, "imperfections," are not easily seen with the naked eye but have a profound effect both structurally and aesthetically.

There with purpose, the brilliance of small imperfections can be found carefully weaved into the blueprints of the Parthenon. The design safeguarded the structure from earthquakes and the settling of the foundation. Water damage from rain and change of seasons were also mitigated by these purposeful *faults*. Planned deformities also add another glorious dimension to its aesthetic appeal as the curvature of the columns offset an optical illusion. The designers likely knew that as you view two parallel lines from afar, or in this case looking up at the citadel, straight lines, like those from the columns, would appear bent. Curving the columns makes the Parthenon appear to the observer as shear perfection.

There are principles in our lives that form our foundation. We build our very existence upon them. We make mistakes, we fall short, we fail. We are imperfect. However, in that experience, we have a power, much like the Parthenon. If our foundation is strong, if the pillars of our life are fortified, then the imperfections can strengthen us and add a beautiful and relatable dimension to our lives that makes our voice aesthetic and pleasing to others. The Parthenon is a magnum opus of the ancient Grecian world. Yet, like the beauty of nature and art, it is in imperfection that true beauty and endurance is refined.

The Japanese word for this concept is *wabi-sabi*. It is an appreciation of and beauty in the imperfect, the aged, the broken, the melancholy. The aesthetics from the perspective of this Japanese term appreciates the rustic beauty of an old barn resting tiredly in an un-mowed field or the fragility of a glistening icicle. Like the superior taste of an aged wine, it delights in the cracking voice of a groom saying his vows to his bride or the love of an elderly man as he places his wrinkled hand on the back of his frail wife to slowly help her on her way. Wabi-sabi denotes that everything is more beautiful when it bares the marks of age, experience, character, and individuality.

At a small theater on Broadway, I caught the production of *Les Misérables* and a glimpse of the glory of precision juxtaposed with imperfection. As a theater buff and actress, I was enraptured by the production; it was the echelon of excellence. Neither talent, stunning sets, nor musical arrangements were what made this the most astounding performing arts experience of my lifetime. It was an imperfection.

The musical advanced through the story of a man, Jean Valjean, whose soul is salvaged through repentance from prison to personhood. He agrees to care for a dying factory worker's illegitimate daughter as his own. He rises in stature and piety, living a quiet life during the pre-revolution era of nineteenth-century France.

During the end of the musical's first act, French students rallying to revolution in a small cafe sing in full force the musical number, "Red and Black." It boasts rousing and powerful drums, pounding music, and motivating lyrics, As the music crescendoed a young man playing the part of Enjoiras, stood upon a chair, on stage, in a rallying cry. Suddenly, unscripted, one of the chair's legs snaped under his weight. The actor collapsed to the floor wincing in real life pain. The music stopped; the actors froze in place. The audience gasped, daring not to exhale.

We were shaken out of the pretense of 1832 France into the reality of twentieth century New York, but only for the briefest of moments. The actor, without missing a beat, leaped to his one good foot, pain still rendered across his face. On the silent stage, he grabbed the chair, smashing it to the ground. With a primal cry he shouted, "La Révolution!" The music started again in full force, and in unison, the audience charged to their feet, erupting in raucous applause and near the point of tears. That one imperfect moment was the force that overtook the production, carrying it all the way to the final bow.

The actor had a foundation of training, talent, experience, and character that gave power to his voice, his art. While we may not know the ins and outs of his road to fame, we can assume that it is like our own journeys, wrought with trials, disappointments, and failures. Because of these, in what could have been certain disaster and possibly the most embarrassing moment of his life, character had him rising to the occasion. When things went wrong, he seized the opportunity.

What I am suggesting is that you engage in the building of a strong foundation. Construct upon it your experiences, imperfect as they may be. Allow yourself a mind-shift that will help you see your imperfections as beauty and strength. From there, fine tune your message, your mode of delivery, then move onward fearlessly.

Like the Parthenon, it all starts with a solid plan and a good foundation. Foundational character traits like faith, truth, love, goodness, joy, peace, kindness, patience, faithfulness, and self-control will help you weather storms. You will be battered, you will make mistakes, your heart will be broken, you will experience moments of embarrassment. Your foundation will shake and scars will form, but if your foundation is sure, you will not fail. Your blemishes will become your beauty.

Secondly, be willing to look past the bill of goods we have been sold concerning "perfection." The Western world has bombarded us with a false idea of beauty. Much of our perception has been carefully programed to sell more products and a manufactured, make-believe idealism. You are fearfully and wonderfully made; you need only be the best *you* that you can be. Finding and sharing your voice will be a lifetime of work. But you need not be the model of perfection to make your voice perfectly heard.

Someone very, very dear to me has battled depression and, in a daily fight to overcome it, he has become irresistibly beautiful. In his vehicle on a rocky cliff some years ago, he contemplated driving off into the angry sea and into oblivion. In the final moments, before he took his last few breaths, his vehicle idled on the bluff, and he made a choice. He chose to live. With courage, he went on to strive to live a better life. That choice started a trajectory that led to something marvelous.

I see him as a superhero fighting an unseen darkness. Having spent a chunk of time isolated and alone, he managed to slowly pull himself out of a dark pit, re-entering the land of the living. He eventually found true love, genuine happiness, and is now building a beautiful life. That darkness may always hound him, trying to drag him downward. It may seek to remind him of his flaws. Yet through it, he has developed a power that few will ever acquire.

Because of this experience in the imperfection of depression, he has an empathy and fortitude that few on earth possess. When devastation strikes those around him, he is the one person who his friends and acquaintances contact. In his love relationship, he is steadfast and caring, careful to not inflict hurt. He knows the ache of heartache and shuns away from inflicting it. The darkness he has lived through helps him to see potential problems, like having superhero X-ray vision. He is someone who has been through hell and will weather those storms of life by your side. He is a Parthenon of strength because of his "imperfections."

A solid foundation is what we need to weather life's storms, endure hardships, and to stand strong like the Parthenon. Perfection is not achievable in this life. The perception of perfection is not relatable to others. Our flaws, faults, and failures are what give character, beauty, and wabi-sabi to our voice. Finding your voice is more than discovering passion, developing talent, and finding a venue. Finding your voice comes from building on a firm foundation made beautiful by the scars of your life experience. It is through the voice of imperfection that your song becomes lovely and relatable to others.

CHAPTER 3:

THE CYCLE OF DOUBT & DEFEAT

Your voice's nemesis

"YELP." THAT WAS all he heard, a very small "yelp." "On the fifteenth of May in the Jungle of Nool, in the heat of the day, in the cool of the pool" it is said that Horton the Elephant, of Dr. Seuss's illustrated children's book, *Horton Hears a Who*, heard "a very faint yelp."[7] No one else in the jungle could hear it, no one else believed it. The entirety of a small, microscopic civilization that lived on an itty-bitty dust speck, resting on a clover flower, was at stake. As the jungle population persecuted Horton and threatened to boil the dust speck, the people of Whoville strove to make enough noise to be heard. It was, in the end, one small voice, from the tiniest of the tiny Whos, that made the difference and saved the day.

Our voice may not feel important or strong or particularly gifted. We can feel like a small Who on a tiny dust speck. That idea gives power to what is called the voice of doubt and defeat. It is the voice that takes your pain, fear, and failure and grants it more power than it really deserves. It can send you spiraling into a cycle of doubt, defeat, and unfulfilled dreams.

The cycle of doubt and defeat is one that many will never escape. When faced with a possibility or an opportunity, failure and fear of failure rise up like the growth of a burning ember. You feed that ember with fear of embarrassment

---

[7]   Dr. Seuss, *Horton hears a Who!*, (Random House, 2020)

and the memory of humiliation, loss, pain, and misery. The ember grows into a fire of doubt. Stunted, you may never allow dreams to play out and never meet your full potential. You succumb to defeat. When the next opportunity arises, you are even less inclined to move forward.

Doubt and fear are protection mechanisms that warn you against pain and failure. Should you choose to succumb to the voice of doubt, it will embolden your conviction that you cannot succeed. Doubt unchallenged is nothing more than faith aimed in the wrong direction. That faith continues to build a stronger case against yourself. Your fears then morph into "fact". Defeat becomes your comfort zone, your reality. If you stay where you are, you will not be called out, you will not be shamed, you will not fail. Yet, you have already failed in your lack of action.

THE CYCLE OF DOUBT AND DEFEAT:

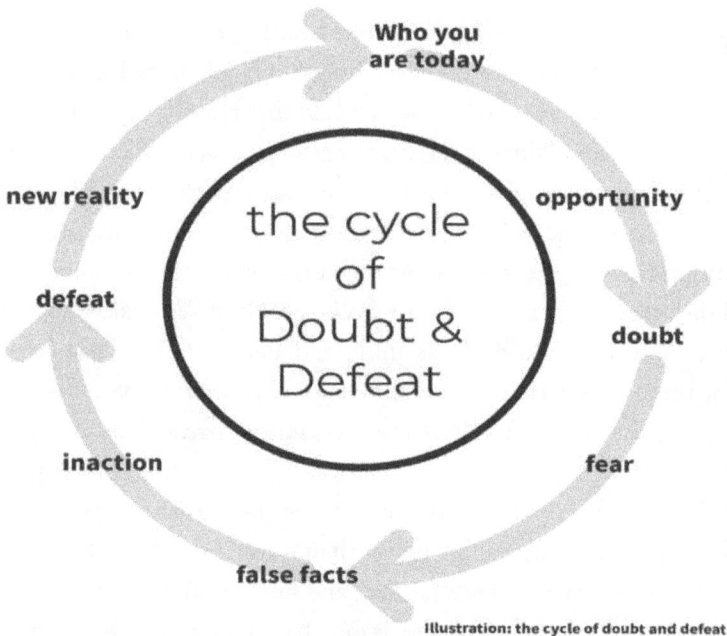

Illustration: the cycle of doubt and defeat

This illustration shows how the cycle of doubt and defeat works against you.

WHO YOU ARE TODAY: Who you are is a result of the choices you have made in the past.

OPPORTUNITY: You will be faced with a new opportunity.

DOUBT: Doubts will arise. Some doubt may be manifested in healthy questions about how to move forward. Some is based on fear of embarrassment, loss, pain, or failure.

FEAR: Fear grows from unconfronted doubts.

FALSE FACTS: To protect yourself, you build a case against yourself and fortify your fear with false facts about how you are unable to move ahead. These are excuses that become your new "truth".

INACTION: Fear can paralyze you, keeping you from moving forward.

NEW REALITY: You have bought into your own bad press. When opportunities present themselves, your case for failure is stronger than your desire to achieve more.

When a reporter asked Thomas Edison, the inventor of the light bulb, how it felt to fail so many times, Edison is said to have replied, "I didn't fail a thousand times. The light bulb was an invention with a thousand steps." Great success is built on failure, frustration, even catastrophe. There are one thousand ways that you will fail, one thousand ways that you are not good enough, one thousand ways that you will never make it. That is, if failure is an option and you operate in the cycle of doubt and defeat. If failure is not an option, then every one of these one thousand setbacks are nothing more than a lesson on how to eventually find your way.

Thomas Edison was not building a light bulb on false hopes and dreams. He pulled upon his experience, education, passion, and training. He took the pain of failure and turned it all into a life lesson to glean from. He broke the cycle of doubt and defeat to find success.

If failure were an option, I would have ridden the rail of defeat right out of my career as a talk show host years ago. After all, as I began my career, talk radio was the epitome of a man's world. "Angry, white, males", was the label given to radio talk show hosts when I started in the business. I was neither angry, white, nor male. Being different, not fitting in, breaking the mold, standing out, and being the odd ball is never easy and can become fodder for the cycle of doubt and defeat. Nothing worthwhile is easy. Nothing. Being a unique person who provides something like no one else, can be your key to success. Thus, being the odd person out can be your greatest advantage.

Perhaps being different gave me insight that my coworkers did not have, but that difference nearly cost me the courage to move forward. Before technology made websites available for everyone and their pet iguanas, individuals, businesses, and television and radio stations did not even conceive of having an internet presence. Yet, I had an idea that could put our radio station on the web in ways that were not yet imagined.

The program director of the big city radio station that I worked for seemed so pious. He sat in his big cushy chair, in his big corner office, with his big picture window, sporting a big, beautiful city view. Across the mahogany desk, yes it too was big, in a small, hard chair, this young talk show host sat. My neck was cranked upward towards this ascended figure as I presented my case for the internet.

Presenting a plan for an internet webpage that I had created using simple code, I was brimming with enthusiasm. My rudimentary page offered a few pictures and simple chat features, client links, and guest information. I navigated the program director through the pages, presenting a vision for my radio show and the station. This fantastic technology could give us better reach and connection with our audience.

What happened next was an "Are you kidding me?" moment. The program director smiled wryly with a hint of disinterest in his eyes and condescension curling up at the corners of his mouth. He put his hand on my knee with a patronizing little, *tap, tap*. He said, "That might be a nice resource for sharing recipes with your little girlfriends, but the world wide web and radio will never mix." His words haunted me for years. So many years later, his words may haunt him now.

At that time, I was dejected. My face heated under frustration and anger. The wind fell from my sails in dismissal, patronization, and misogyny. Today, however, every radio station from New York City to "Podunkville, U.S.A." has a webpage. My resumé boasts top level accomplishments in my field, and I have, since that time, created many webpages, including the one for this book and subsequent classes, www.findyourvoice.fun. This man's lack of vision stunted his career. The last I heard of that former boss, he was out of the radio industry altogether and managing a lube and oil change franchise somewhere in suburban Washington State. His career in radio topped out. Every lesson learned through my embarrassment and defeat became wisdom in the bank for me to draw upon. Eventually I cashed in to build my future.

As children we dream of what we might be someday. We fantasize about the impractical. We pretend to be something we are not. We believe in the impossible. We have faith that our *yelp* can be heard. If we are lucky, some of that enthusiasm makes its way into adulthood. It is as though we could take off like a vehicle racing with fever down the highway, enthusiasm filling our tank. It is the positive faith in ourselves that propels us. The mix of childlike faith and life experience is the mixing of the impossible into a masterpiece of the probable.

Sitting in his big office, my ex-boss struck me as the voice of experience, power, and know-how. He turned out to be a brick wall to my hopes, a possible dead end to my zeal. I could have easily fallen into the trap of doubt and defeat, just existing and never expressing. I might have succumbed to the perceived voice of reason and experience, fearful of the inner yelp beckoning me towards more. The faith that I pulled upon propelled me forward. The practical reality I faced made me examine the obstacles. Together they gave direction for realistic navigation.

An experience, like mine, with a brick wall like my program director, can take the wind out of your sails, as well. People are creatures of comfort; they like to play it safe. Like a child who has been burned by the heat of the stove, we recoil, we feel shame. What if that child never again approached the stove? He may never become the chef he was meant to be. Those willing to take chances, tweak their approaches, learn from mistakes, and never give up, are those who become change in the world. It is they who will see their dreams come true.

There are any number of reasons that you are engaged in this book. You have a passion and need direction. Giving a good interview, starting a podcast, or public speaking may be your desire. Perhaps your voice in the workplace is hindered. Disadvantages may have kept you from effective communication. Each of these can be starting points, or they can feed into the diseases of doubt and defeat, plaguing your potential.

Sir Cecil Walter Hardy Beaton was a twentieth century British photographer and designer. Shockingly, he was mostly self-taught in his craft. He faced his share of scrutiny as he approached his skill from a different perspective. With bravery, brilliant innovation, and imagination, he greatly influenced art in photography and was featured in many leading periodicals. He changed how pictures could capture the moments of our life. Cecil Beaton was innovative in creating set designs that won him three Academy Awards, including one for *My Fair Lady* in 1964. There is also another distinguishing attribute of Cecil's. He is the creator of my favorite life quote.

"Be daring, be different, be impractical, be anything that will assert integrity of purpose and imaginative vision against the play-it-safers, the creatures of the commonplace, the slaves of the ordinary." For me, this encapsulates the spirit needed to break through the ordinary and achieve what many will never reach in their lifetime, the extraordinary.

As we work to meet your potential by finding and expressing your voice, you will be encouraged to reach for the extraordinary. Do not just break the cycle of defeat and doubt, use it for ultimate success. Your personality, full of quirks and distinctions, can drive your learning and communication techniques. For some personality types, the thought of the impractical and daring is unsettling, the ease of defeat is lulling. Do not be deterred. It takes all learning types, all communication styles, and all personalities to make a better world. Your voice is needed.

"When you doubt your power, you give power to your doubt." These words spoken by French novelist and playwright Honoré De Balzac are indicative of the power of the cycle of doubt and defeat that manifests in each of us. Often, it can manifest itself in its own devilish way with agitation or anger. Pride can be the mask we don to hide our fears. Arrogance or indifference can intimidate our frightened inner child. Intellect and logic can become tools we use to justify inaction. Regardless of the symptoms, the disease of doubt and fear is still the culprit of complacency.

There is a beautiful balance between the improbable and the possible. What it takes to tip you to the right side is a change in belief. Theoretical physicist Albert Einstein is credited with saying, "The definition of insanity is doing the same thing over and over and expecting different results." If you keep doing the same thing over and over, you will always have the same results in life. You have invested in yourself enough to read this far. If you want different results, read on.

CHAPTER 4:

FEAR FACTOR

Overcoming the enemy of fear

F EAR FACTOR WAS an American reality television show that aired from 2001-2006 until one outlandish stunt forced the show into immediate cancelation. Contestants on the show faced their worst fears and phobias. If they made it through a gauntlet of challenges, their prize was a $50,000 award. The rounds of competition were traumatizing, dangerous, and often stomach-turning. Hanging from helicopters, being entombed in a coffin with live rats, eating sheep's eyeballs or live crawling creatures, each season they upped the horror element. There was, however, one challenge that pushed the envelope so far that it brought the show to a screeching halt. On the episode in question, participants played a typical lawn game of horseshoes. There was something quite atypical about this familiar game, however. As they tossed the projectiles, they were sprayed down with donkey urine and semen. Some drank the mixture. The media frenzy and outrage that ensued was the final nail in the coffin for the show.

The same reason people were glued to *Fear Factor* is the reason they also tuned out in outrage. We live vicariously as we watch, and there comes a moment when fear gets the better of us. Witnessing fear and failure is like observing a train wreck, you cannot help but watch. However, sometimes you must look away. Even though provocative, it feels safe to watch someone else face fears and challenges from the comfort of your living room couch. There is a sense that we have empathically experienced something when really, we are simply observers. While engineered to strive and prevail, we also possess a need for self-preservation.

Self-preservation and comfort are necessary. We are wired to be suspicious to varying degrees. This is helpful. The fear mechanism is there to protect us from harm. Fear shields us from our own stupidity. It encourages us to be prepared. It inspires us to become masterful. However, it can also paralyze us even when viewing someone else's experience.

Neuroscience has shown that trepidation and uncertainty feel similar to failure. "Fear of failure (also called atychiphobia) is the feeling of dread that many people experience when approaching a project or a life goal. It is a sense of insecurity that interferes with someone's thoughts, emotions, and actions. When kept in check, fear of failure can be positive, but it can easily grow out of control and become paralyzing."[8] Our minds surrender to defeat before we ever begin the challenge. This is why we enjoy standing on the sidelines and watching as others play the game and take the risks.

My cousin is a legendary drummer who would often tour with world-renowned headliners. My cousin's favorite uncle was my daddy, "Uncle Pete". One fall, in my youth, my cousin was on tour with one of the greatest singer-songwriters of all time, Bob Dylan. Dylan was scheduled to play in Seattle, where I grew up, and my family was invited to the show. On this visit, as we walked from my cousin's hotel to the Paramount theater, he said, "I want to introduce you to someone." We approached a man I assumed was homeless. His scraggly beard, worn jeans, and T-shirt were partially illuminated by the lamppost he leaned casually against. The figure was talking about Jesus to a college kid from the nearby University of Washington. The homeless looking guy was actually Bob Dylan.

Bob was kind-hearted, endearing, and seemed genuinely interested in my family. He turned to me and asked, "So you're a little singer?" I replied with a vigorous, "Yes, and I know your songs!" I proceeded to sing something from his latest album. My father squeezed my hand trying to hush me. He felt that

---

[8] Tanya J. Peterson, "Fear of Failure: Causes & 5 Ways to Cope with Atychiphobia." Choosing Therapy, January 24, 2022 https://www.choosingtherapy.com/fear-of-failure.

I might be overstepping my bounds. Children have a sense of boldness that is often lost in grown-up years. Bob, however, smiled and chuckled at the impromptu performance. He invited me to come up on stage at the concert later to sing with the backup singers. Yes! I was twelve years old, and I was more excited than I could ever find words to express.

Later came. I stood backstage and peered out around the heavy, red velvet curtains of the theater. My body froze as I beheld a seemingly endless audience of seats quickly filling with people. Bob must have seen the paralyzing fear on my face as he asked in his unique Bob Dylan voice, "Hey, you ready?" The word, "No!" was in my head but nothing would come out of my mouth as I choked on my own breath. Nor could I move. The most amazing opportunity, perhaps a once in a lifetime moment, and I could not muster the courage to seize it! That is until Bob Dylan, himself, said something to me that changed my perspective forever.

Bob confessed something I will never forget. "Ah, don't worry! Before every concert, about a half an hour before, I'm in the bathroom with diarrhea. But I get out there anyway and it's all good." Take a moment to ponder that. My stage fright was demolished in an instant. At the tender age of twelve, I was given something that has stayed with me all the days of my life. If I was not in the bathroom with diarrhea, I felt better than Bob. I would be fine. What I was really experiencing was the realization that Bob Dylan, as famous and amazing as he is, is just human. Like me, he has talents, abilities, and yes, fears. We are all made of the same stuff. If one man can overcome his fear, then why can't I?

I walked out on the stage, sandwiched between three large, beautiful black women with the richest most glorious voices I ever heard. I sang along, in a likely unplugged microphone, and walked away with a victorious memory. It was an experience that helped shape the rest of my life.

Atychiphobia, the fear of failure, is the fear that becomes stronger than our desire to succeed, pilfering our future goals. Every one of us stands toe to toe, at one time or another, with this monster. Yet, those who truly succeed find something that helps defeat the beast. The bigger the beast, the greater the success. It may just take a leap of faith.

Indiana Jones, in the movie *Indiana Jones and the Last Crusade*, has to take a leap of faith to complete his quest. His father, played by Sean Connery, has been fatally wounded by a gun shot. Indiana has to run a gauntlet of challenges through a cavernous archeological find to find the legendary Holy Grail. The Grail was said to grant life to those who drink from it and is the only hope for saving his father.

One of the challenges is a literal leap of faith. Indiana stands on the cliff of an endless chasm. "Impossible," he says, sweat beaded across his body and fear darkening his eyes. "Nobody can jump this." His father shrieks out in pain as someone yells out, "Indy, Indy you must hurry!" Indiana Jones, the brave hero, is paralyzed not knowing what to do. He suddenly realizes, "It's a leap of faith!" His father, emboldening him with his own faith, whispers, "You must believe boy, you must believe."[9]

Indiana Jones is left with no luck, clever plans, nor acts of heroism drawn from intellect and ability. He puts his hand on his heart, closes his eyes, and takes a deep resigning breath. Toes over the edge, he lifts a leg and steps forward into the unknown. As you watch this scene for the first time, your breath stops, the music swells, and you see Indiana land on a narrow bridge that was invisible from his previous vantage point. Relieved, he makes his way safely across the bridge to the chamber on the other side.

If we can change our perspective, the impossible seems more probable and a way forward may come into view. We must find a way through the forest of doubt to find the clearing of victory. Failure need not be an end, but part of the method. As the old adage goes, "if at first you don't succeed, try, try again." Sometimes we must take the risk of failure, trying and trying again, because standing still is not an option.

Think of others who have learned that failure is not the end, but part of the process. Robert F. Kennedy said, "Only those who dare to fail greatly can ever achieve greatly." Motivational speaker Denis Waitley said that "Failure should be our teacher, not our undertaker. Failure is delay, not defeat. It is a temporary detour, not a dead end. Failure is something we can avoid only by saying nothing, doing nothing, and being nothing." Winston Churchill

---

[9] Spielberg, Stephen, director. 1998. *Indiana Jones and the Last Crusade.* Paramount Pictures.

once said, "Success is not final, failure is not fatal; it is the courage to continue that counts."

Life is a process full of successes and failures. Success and failure are two sides of the same coin. One side is incomplete without the other. If it were not for the tenacious spirit of Thomas Edison and his willingness to embrace defeat a thousand times, you might not be reading this by the illumination of a light bulb.

Finding your voice is a process that every human is capable of. It starts with a deep dive into your soul to find your foundation. Next, we tune into the desires of the heart and its unique calling. This is the vision, the potential work of art that can float like an unformed dream in your head. You then cultivate your strengths, talents, and skills to make the dream a reality. These are the paints and brushes of your masterpiece. You find the venue, an outlet to present your voice. This is your canvas. With persistence and dedication, your life's work has purpose and soon becomes a work of art.

We seem to be programmed for purpose. A Bible memory verse from my youth comes to mind. "For I know the plans I have for you," declares the Lord, "plans to prosper you and not to harm you, plans to give you hope and a future."(Jer. 29:11) The idea that you were forged with a purpose is compelling, but it is not an inoculation against fear or failure. With a change in perspective, however, fear and failure can morph from our nemesis to our school master in our quest to create a life masterpiece to share with the world.

CHAPTER 5:

FAILURE IS NOT AN OPTION

How the heroes do it

YOU CANNOT EAT an egg without breaking its shell; you cannot taste success without breaking through your fears. Your potential may lie behind a protective shell that shields you. Do not fear the breakage. It's part of life. The cycle of doubt and defeat are a breeding ground for real success. That is, if you can dare to go beyond your current reality and learn from, rather than run from, fear.

Think for a moment of what man has been able to achieve. We have broken the confines of perceived reality in space travel and technological advancement. These wonders prove that what we once only dreamed of, we now have achieved. The long journey from pondering the night sky to traveling beyond the stars has been characterized by much doubt, defeat, and fear, but also perseverance and faith.

In the year 1610, observations of the night sky, our moon's craters, Jupiter's moons, and phases of Venus, were seen by man for the very first time via telescopic observation. After gazing at these objects, Galileo said, "I have observed four planets, neither known nor observed by any one of the astronomers before my time... observed a few days ago, by the help of a telescope devised by me, through God's grace first enlightening my mind."[10]

---

[10] Galileo Gaelilei, *The Greatest Astonishment.* (1610)

That first step of an enlightened mind is not something to merely gloss over. Galileo Galilei faced many brick wall issues, a cycle of doubt, and defeat that would be familiar to us today. Funding issues, jealousy from his peers, difficulty with the patent process, and close-minded people who feared challenges to conventional ideas were all obstacles he faced. He even dealt with the failure of some of his own hypotheses and was under house imprisonment at the end of his life for his support of Copernicus's theory that the Earth revolved around the sun. This enraged some of the scientific and religious thinkers of the day. His work was confined to the *Index Librorum Prohibitorum*, the list of forbidden books of the church. No prison of the earth, however, could confine a mind that is enlightened by God's grace.

By the 1950s, we could view, via telescope, only ".001% of the entire observable extent of the universe."[11] This, according to astrophysicist and founder of Reasons to Believe, Dr. Hugh Ross. Ross, in an interview on my podcast, went on to say that "Today we are getting close to 100%."[12]

As our observations of space have grown, thanks to many of the contributions of men like Galileo, so has our vision. By the 1800s, Jules Verne had fictionalized the dream of extraterrestrial travel to the moon. Imagination took flight as the first manned space flight took place in 1961. Soon thereafter, the first moon landing occurred in 1969. Today we are planning a manned operation to Mars. Vision, enlightenment, and hope always move us beyond the current reality.

In the mid-1960s the American television show *Star Trek* birthed into our psyche devices and dreams that have made their way from vision to daily life. The images once fictionalized on our television screens are today's realities and are part of our daily routine. Laptop computers, touch screens, real life communicators that we know as cell phones, and telepresence technology or video conference calls; the fantasy of yesterday is the technology of today. These realities were birthed from imagination by the impractical and daring individuals who ventured to believe dreams could happen. They broke the cycle of doubt and defeat.

Never let someone else's expectation of failure define you. There are many people who feel that they are disadvantaged, discriminated against, and set

---

[11] *MyMichelleLive Podcast*, "Strange signals from the center of the universe." Host, Michelle Mendoza; Guest, Dr. Hugh Ross, Reasons to Believe, aired October 19, 2021. http://mymichellelive.com

[12] Ibid

up for failure. They will try to convince you that you too are less able or less privileged. Do not let that be the reason that you succumb to defeat and doubt. You may have to work harder to succeed in some areas, but it will make you stronger and harder working, with astounding endurance.

In my radio job, I sometimes fought an uphill climb as a woman. There was a time that if you wanted to advance, you needed to be part of the "good ol' boy's club". Decisions and promotions often happened while the guys went out after work to the strip club, a place that female employees were not invited and had little interest in going. The environment created doubt and defeat. I was on the outside. I doubted that I could ever break into the inner circle. I doubted that I could be seen as worthy. I was different and doubted that I could fit in. I questioned my worth. My lower middle-class, half-ethnic background did not afford me the privilege of others, or so I told myself. The doubt nearly led to defeat.

Doubt built a case for failure. It became a list of why I could not, why I would fail, and why I should not put myself out there to be embarrassed again. It cataloged a myriad of reasons why I was not good enough or experienced enough, what the insurmountable obstacles were, and why I needed to play it safe. In the end, it was the excuse for why I simply could not. We become incapable of seeing past the roadblocks. In defeat, we throw up our hands and leave success to those we see as better qualified. But what if failure were no longer an option?

The first step to breaking the cycle of doubt and defeat is, surprisingly, the choice to face doubt and defeat head on. The cycle of doubt and defeat is a real part of our human experience. It is much like the cycle of grief when we have experienced the gut-wrenching loss of a loved one. We go through different stages of shock, denial, pain, guilt, depression, acceptance, and hope. We must walk through the pain of each to experience healing. We must live through the stages, sometime many times over, before relief and recovery come to us. It may be called the grieving process, but it may well be considered the healing process. It is not easy, but it is worth the hope.

Near Houston, Texas, at NASA's Space Center, your tour will take you past the marvels and breathtaking innovations of man's quest in the exploration of space. You can stand behind a worn wooden podium that President John F. Kennedy stood behind on September 12, 1962, at Rice Stadium, as he delivered what we now know as, "The Moon Speech."

President Kennedy's words are a powerful motivation for those who would stand on the precipice of the seemingly impossible, and those of us who need a nudge as we try something new. He said, "We choose to go to the moon. We choose to go to the moon in this decade and do the other things, not because they are easy, but because they are hard, because that goal will serve to organize and measure the best of our energies and skills, because that challenge is one that we are willing to accept, one we are unwilling to postpone, and one which we intend to win."[13]

Those words are a ruler we can use to measure ourselves against something challenging. Is this something that you are willing to accept, something you are unwilling to postpone, and something which you intend to conquer? Now, let your fear, doubt, and unsurety become the hills you climb to get there. Let them warn you of potential problems. If you fail, redirect, and try again with the mindset that failure is not an option.

The tag line for the 1995 film, *Apollo 13*, is, "Failure is not an option." It is also an unofficial motto of NASA. The movie was based on the eighth crewed mission in the Apollo space program. The mission was a near disaster, as an oxygen tank in the service module failed two days into the voyage. The movie gives us a voyeurs look at the heart-pounding calamity the crew faced as they calculated and executed a loop around the moon. We breathed a heavy sigh of relief as they eventually brought themselves safely home to Earth. The crew refused to fail.

According to urban legend, the phrase, "Failure is not an option," arose from an interview the script writers had with Flight Controller Jerry Bostick. As they compiled information for the film on the Mission Control culture and people of the mission, Bostick was asked, "Weren't there times when everybody, or at least a few people, just panicked?" Bostick's answer was unfaltering, "No, when bad things happened, we just calmly laid out all the options, and failure was not one of them."[14]

---

[13] John F. Kennedy, 1962. *Special Message to Congress on Urgent National Needs (The Moon Speech).* (May 25, 1962)

[14] Aytekin Tank,. "'Failure Is Not an Option.' What Apollo 13 Teaches Entrepreneurs About Problem-Solving". Entrepreneur. Feb 24, 2021, https://www.entrepreneur.com/leadership/failure-is-not-an-option-what-apollo-13-teaches/364660

If failure is an option, you will more than likely take that option and achieve failure. If failure is not an option, you will find a way to change defeat into delight. These are the tools that put people on the moon in the face of uncertainty. They did it not because it was easy but because it was hard. The challenge was one that they were willing to accept, one they were unwilling to postpone, and one which they intended to win. Let this be our rallying cry.

These are instruments successful people have used, time and again, to overcome defeat and doubt. On your journey, you will experience dead-end situations that can either defeat or define you. You will be humiliated. You will be devastated. You will be wounded. You will be dejected. But you need not be destroyed. This is where you take your pain and turn it into your passions and success.

An unlikely candidate for success, Katherine Johnson, was a mother, a widow, and a black minority in a time when any of these factors would be a strike against success in the early days of the American space program. Johnson was also the mathematician who calculated and analyzed the flight paths of many spacecrafts in her more than three decades with NASA. She was one of the subjects of the 2016 film, *Hidden Figures*. Katherine Johnson faced segregation issues, discrimination, and a fight for recognition.

During her tenure, Johnson earned respect and success. She also earned astronaut John Glenn's unaltered trust. It is said that as computers had been programmed with equations for orbital trajectory, Glenn, not trusting glitchy computers, said, "Get the girl," referring to Johnson. Katherine Johnson ran the numbers by hand and helped secure a trajectory for the flight. She died in 2020 but not without seeing a multi-decade career result in a flourish of space discoveries and possibilities met. Katherine Johnson received numerous awards and honors for her work, including the Presidential Medal of Freedom in 2015. Johnson helped us to journey to the beyond.

Failure was not an option for Katherine Johnson and others who dared to dream beyond doubt and defeat. Johnson stands as a hero to this day, having faced fearful challenges while remaining strong. Space is a fitting backdrop for achieving the impossible. Space seems to be without limit. We are, ourselves, only limited by the confines that we allow. We bind our own trajectory or we ourselves unleash it.

CHAPTER 6:

STRENGTHEN YOUR SYSTEM

Exposure increases our superpower

TS THEME WAS "Lime in da Coconut Party", a local gathering meant to bring a feel of beach and sun to a cool, soggy February weekend. Partygoers wore aloha shirts and leis. Tropical music and vibrant colors filled the small urban house party. Fruity drinks abounded.

It was early 2020. This event turned out to be America's first COVID-19 super spreader. It ominously took place in the Northwest corner of the United States, as *coronavirus* and *COVID* first entered our collective vocabulary. Party guests were oblivious to the lurking virus until it hit. For some it hit hard. More than a half-dozen people who attended showed symptoms within the week. National news picked up the story within days. It was thought that is was the asymptomatic that spread the virus unaware. Like a wildfire, news and fear of the outbreak spread on the party page on social media, gathering hundreds of comments, questions, concerns.

I was invited to that party. By chance, my schedule was just too full to make it that night. I attended an earlier get-together hosted by a friend, then had to rush away for media coverage of our local Major League Rugby team. I sent my regrets. Many of my friends were in attendance, many of my close friends contracted COVID-19. All were unaware that someone there had and was spreading the virus. Though no one who contracted the virus died, I still felt as though I had dodged a huge coronavirus bullet.

The world soon went into full-on panic mode. You may recall the days before our typical way of life took a drastic change as we entered the COVID era. I sipped coffee at a local coffee shop on the eve of my state's lockdowns. I was soaking in the last moments of normalcy, thinking to myself, "The world will look very different tomorrow." There was a collective feeling, among many, that life may never be the same. Suddenly, there were runs on supplies of toilet paper and hand sanitizer. Social and physical distancing ensued. People were confined in their homes, unable to leave but for imperative travel. All but a few select businesses were closed as authorities chose who was and who was not "essential."

While I sat, imprisoned in my home, feeling as though I was under house arrest, friends who had contracted COVID and subsequently recovered, lived their lives in confident connection. They would gather for walks, hikes, and meals. They felt that they had it, survived it, and with what we knew about natural immunity, were less likely to get it again. These friends, in the early days of the pandemic, had a fearlessness in the face of reinfection.

Our emotional system and our immune system share a powerful similarity. They both become stronger after surviving invasion. Defeat and doubt are the emotional pathogens that assault our psyche and can sicken our soul. As with a virus, many may succumb to invasion and never truly recover. Our bodies and souls are ideally designed to take attack, to be wounded, and then heal themselves. With the right help, we can be even stronger than before the invasion.

I started to understand the miracle of healing and strengthening when my son was but a baby. A new mother, I dressed and changed, fed, cleaned, and outright adored Joshua like he was a living doll. I was obsessed with sterilizing everything in the home to protect my child from harm. I would have sterilized everyone who entered the home if I could have. Imagine a family in white hazmat suits as people sat down for dinner. Though I did not go that far, I was near obsession where germs were concerned. Despite my efforts, Joshua would often get ear infections, a runny nose, cough, and other symptoms of illness.

Friends, who had a child just one week to the day older than my son, had no such problems with their child's immune system. Their baby would crawl on dirty floors and gnaw on his father's steel-toed work boot like a teething toy. He never got sick. I learned from that experience that babies need to be exposed to dirt and germs to train their brand-new immune systems. My son's little immune system had virtually nothing to fight against to strengthen it.

I would not recommend letting your baby chew on a parent's shoes to strengthen their immune system, but I do recommend staying clear of near obsessive-compulsive tendencies that overprotect you and your loved ones from unseen harm. As I changed my outlook, my baby's health greatly improved.

This is similar to our body's muscles, which need to be used and worked out to become strong. When we use our muscles, it can hurt. If we try to protect our muscles from that sore ache by not using them, our muscles will go into atrophy and become useless. We are born with an immune system that needs to be exercised. Our bodies learn how to make antibodies to fight off future exposure and then become stronger. We additionally have human psyches that become stronger when exposed to challenge.

More than a year after the super spreader party, I contracted COVID-19. The survivability for most who are in non-high-risk groups may be high, but it was not a virus to take lightly. My muscles and joints ached, taste and smell waned, my hair thinned, and I spent two weeks in bed. I was blessed to have had nearly two years of radio and online virus specific content from my show to fall back on. I interviewed doctors and health practitioners who were on the front lines of battling COVID. It gave me an inside line. I was stocked up with homeopathic remedies, the right vitamins, and natural viral protocols to battle the disease. I had already abandoned refined sugars and food choices that rape immune systems. I fed my body immune building super foods. I dosed up on vitamins C and D. My relief was swift, and recovery complete because I gave my body what it needed. I did not require additional medical intervention, thankfully. No, it was not fun, but in the end, my immune system was stronger because of the experience.

Now liken these experiences to our soul. Doubt and defeat sicken our soul. We try desperately to avoid exposure, to stave off the hurt. Doubt and defeat are pathogens which, once defeated, strengthen us in the end. Natural exposure or minimal exposure through vaccines are how we introduce viral challenges to our system. Where emotional pathogens are concerned, we need exposure to build up our souls. Simply put, to conquer the cycle of doubt and defeat we must be exposed to doubt and defeat.

You've heard the adage, "No pain no gain." Without true pain, there is no struggle, no strengthening. We are unrelatable and thus ineffective in our communication. It is our pain, fears, failures, and experience that makes us wise. It connects us with the very real needs of a world in the midst of its own struggles. You have a message that others have a need to glean from. That message is only relatable because of your life's challenges. It is in the striving that your lessons have been learned, your talent honed, and your passion proven. These are the musical notes of your voice's song that must be sung.

If you could metaphorically look at a piece of music under a microscope, a beautiful emotional piece of music that moves you, you would find complexity. Some of the most celebrated compositions of man have a mix of timbre, tempo, pitch, and dynamics. The piece will build, rise, and fall. In the mixture of this intricacy, there is both consistency and variation. What you would not see is the life experience and emotion of the composer that makes the piece what it is.

One of the most moving pieces of music in human history is as familiar to most of us as a Christmas sugar cookie. It is "The Grand Pas de Deux" of *The Nutcracker Suite*, a masterpiece of the nineteenth century Russian composer Pyotr Ilyich Tchaikovsky. Ritualistically performed during the holidays by ballet companies across the planet and played in every department store, holiday gathering, and bus station as Christmas nears, this exquisite piece has been well-deemed as the finest music in the whole ballet. Tucked within the nearly five-minute score, you hear beauty, darkness, struggle, light, victory, and hope. But this yuletide treasure was almost never written.

It is said that Tchaikovsky asked to be released from the commission that employed him to write the Nutcracker. He feared that he could not translate the writings of this fairy tale into a musical ballet score. It seemed an impossible task. He may have felt ill equipped, despite his great talent.

Tragedy set in and what could have defeated him, instead spurred him on, inspiring him to compose beauty from sorrow. Aleksandra, "Sasha", his beloved little sister died of cholera as Tchaikovsky was departing for a series of concerts in America. As the steamboat inched its way across the great ocean, Tchaikovsky is said to have considered the utopian-like childhood of Sasha and the unbearable pain in her passing. From this experience, he poured his heart into his work. Tchaikovsky shared his voice in music and saturated the world with a timeless piece of beauty that shortens my breath and brings a tear to my eyes at every hearing. Only from the struggle of the human experience can come such wonderous works of art.

The concept of the masterpiece that you truly are cannot be overstated. Nor can we underestimate the composition that your voice can create. Tchaikovsky weathered the negative and produced from it a positive and enduring achievement. The brilliant secret is refinement in fire and beauty that emerges from the ashes.

How does beauty emerge from the ashes of our failings? It is in the overcoming. We have already addressed the cycle of doubt and defeat as well as fear and fear of failure. Yet, should we choose to overcome and learn from our failings, we strengthen our system. We become better, stronger, wiser, and more equipped to fight off future attacks of doubt and defeat.

FACE THE FAILURE

You may have hit a brick wall. You may be entering uncharted territory. It is okay to take time to meditate on what happened. Feel the anger of defeat. Burn in embarrassment. Mourn your impasse. Live through the pain but consider yourself a visitor there. Do not buy real estate and build a home to abide in forever. You will be stronger and wiser for this experience.

FACE THE FEAR

Fear is the warning sign of possible disaster. Fear can be something we learn from or it can become faith set in a negative direction that paralyzes us. Allow fear and doubt to become your tutors. Ask yourself, "What am I afraid of?" Look for solutions that can help to turn your mountains into climbable adventures. Learn from others who have walked this path.

FACE REALITY

Perception changes the cycle of doubt and defeat into steps for strengthening. Take time to chart what your life would be like if you give in to fear. If you play it safe, what will the next few years look like? Does it take you closer to your dreams and goals? If not, be willing to change your reality. From the struggle of healing comes your strongest power, your voice.

She was considered one of the first black American women to have served in the military. A scout, a spy, and a nurse for the Union Army during the American Civil War, she served as a fierce guerrilla soldier. As a conductor on the Underground Railroad, she brought many a slave to freedom. Her name was Harriet Tubman.

She was born into slavery. By age five, the age most of us were learning ABCs and coloring pictures in kindergarten, she was already rented out by her owners as a domestic servant. Physical violence was part of her daily life and it resulted in permanent physical damage that she endured all her days.

The abuse strengthened her resolve to make a difference. One morning, when she was a young child, she sustained five brutal lashings before breakfast. The scars remained on her back for the rest of her life. Again, when just twelve years old, she put herself between her master and a fellow slave who had tried to escape. Her master, enraged, struck her in the head with a two-pound weight. The trauma left her with lifelong health issues.

Tubman and two of her siblings eventually escaped to the North, aided by white and black abolitionists. Harriet Tubman survived the dangerous trek to find herself a free woman. Before her laid a life of possibilities and choices.

She, however, wished for something greater than her own freedom. It was the passion of her heart to have freedom be a reality for her family, friends, and other slaves. Her desire was to be part of the solution.

Harriet Tubman had to conquer doubt and defeat. She had to face the fears of being caught, the doubts in her abilities as an uneducated former slave, her weakness in stature as a woman, and the limitations caused by her permanent injuries. She could not ignore these obvious realities. She could not pretend that the impediments did not exist. Nor could she sit back in comfort and freedom and do nothing to help those still in bondage. So, Harriet Tubman faced down doubt and possible defeat believing in something greater. It was then that she found her voice.

For ten years, she traveled from North to South and back again, making over a dozen trips, facing unbelievable danger, and guiding dozens of people to freedom. She lived with a $40,000 bounty on her head, which in today's currency would be $1.25 million. Tubman was never caught and never lost a single passenger on her Underground Railroad endeavors.

She lives on through history as a hero, but was just a person, like you and I, who dared to dream big. She found the courage to face fear and failure, doubt and defeat. The pain and personal defeat brought on from years of slavery, lack of education, dehumanizing cruelty, physical abuse could have sickened her soul like a virus. Instead, she used the experience to become relevant to others and to strengthen her resolve. Hardship empowered her to use her voice to tell a story that others, to this day, strain to hear.

Whatever you have experienced in life, whatever challenges you overcame in the development of your skills, they give power to your voice as you express yourself to others. Your impact on the world will be in direct relation to your ability to remember, connect with, and overcome your doubt, defeat, and drawbacks. When it comes time to share your voice and passion, it will be these very things that make you relatable to your audience. Whether you are looking to help strengthen women after the pains of domestic violence or teach guitar lessons, your struggles and victories are the lessons that your audience will benefit from.

Harriet Tubman once said, "Every great dream begins with a dreamer. Always remember, you have within you the strength, the patience, and the passion to reach for the stars to change the world."[15] When remembering her life story and struggles, that statement takes on so much more power. Tubman overcame and became more resilient in the end. We too, in overcoming, develop a superpower that can propel our voice.

---

[15] Harriet Tubman Monument, Accessed October 20, 2021. https://www.harriet-tubmanmonument.com.

CHAPTER 7:

NEVER GIVE UP, NEVER SURRENDER

A superhero's mantra

TWO TIMID, TEENAGE girls, one with a full head gear of braces on her teeth, enveloping her tiny head, sat before me. I had volunteered my time to teach an elective dramatic arts class at a private high school. The very conservative school held strict rules and rigid dress codes. I thought the children would welcome a creative outlet, and I was eager to share my passion and my voice with the kids. Instead of a booming class, wall-to-wall seats filled with eager little learners, only two shy, teen girls graced my classroom.

Every person has a gift and a voice. My goal with my two young students was not to change them. It was not to make them more like me or more like some popular media star, but to nurture the voice already within them. My aim was to teach them to find and bring out their own voice. It was my desire that they discover the courage to share that voice with the world. Both trained with me in poetry reading, dramatic dialogue, and oral argument. We picked and wrote pieces that brought out their true character, passions, and abilities. We perfected their natural delivery.

Even at a young age, a person can pull from life experiences, fears, and failure. As we age, the treasures of life knowledge enrich us. The girls gave presentations and performances birthed from topics that were close to home, painful, poignant, and meaningful. They had passions that ran deep within them. They dealt with issues like abortion, fear of eternity, and finding humor in a need to be heard.

One of the girls had a heart issue that could have ended her life before birth. She took very personally the value of human life and wrote a compelling oral argument on the issue of abortion. She found the words and questions on the topic flowed powerfully and thoughtfully from the troves of her fervor. She delved deeply into the opposing views and facts to better present her thoughts. She sympathized with those who thought differently. She researched stories of children with issues, much like her own. She shed more than a few tears as the process enriched and grew her. You might imagine how much depth it gave her performance.

The girls competed in different categories of performing arts at the state level of high school competition. They were nervous but confident. Both took first place in every event they entered. Upon hearing the news of their victory, the entire school was stunned. Other children became excited; the light came on. They started believing that perhaps, they too, could find and express their own voices. The next year my class was brimming with students burning with a desire to find and share their voices. The astonishing conversion of two, seemingly timid girls into awe inspiring dramatic wonders motivated others to learn the secrets that I am now sharing with you.

One of the students the following year was a boy named Dean. Dean's passion was to one day become a minister. The event he picked for competition, subsequently, was preaching. The problem was that Dean's delivery was as dry as unbuttered, stale, burnt toast.

As his teacher and coach, I chided and encouraged him to engage his audience and build interest. His only response was to gaze at me with the appearance of *Mad* magazine's Alfred E. Newman. With big ol' ears sticking out, and a look of puzzlement on his face, he asked, "What could be more interesting than the word of God?"

Dean's failure was in an inability to connect and effectively communicate his voice in a way that would entice others to listen. He made the mistake of thinking that if a message is important enough, people will pay attention. Martin Blackwell is credited with saying that, "The mind can absorb no more than the seat can endure." Sitting through a dry sermon, no matter how much truth is jam-packed into it, will lose the audience and will certainly not score many points in a high school dramatic arts competition.

We had Dean test his preaching skills on the class. Every time someone started staring off into space, zoning out, doodling, or yawning, I humorously threw a dry, soft sponge in Dean's direction. Midway through his presentation, Dean's stoic stance broke. He started to laugh, uncontrollably. He stopped his sermon asking for help, "Okay, I get it. What do I do?" Dean realized that if he continued on this track, he would be on the road to communication failure. He dared to admit and embrace defeat and imagine change. This is what we call the seek enlightenment step.

Dean had a breakthrough. He faced doubt and defeat by asking for help. He was enlightened. He realized that doing the same thing over and over and over again will never result in a different outcome. Dean sought help, found his center, his passion, and tools for success. Then he followed it all up with action.

What was Dean passionate about? What could connect him with others and make his message, his voice, relatable? It was baseball. When quoting Bible verses, Dean was as robotic as Robot B-9 from the classic television series *Lost in Space*. "Danger, Will Robinson." Something happened, however, when he started quoting baseball stats. While talking about designated hitter, seven-time MLB All-Star, five-time Silver Slugger, and two-time batting champion, Edgar Martinez, Dean lit up like a firecracker. He tuned into that passion and incorporated it into his presentation.

Dean preached on knowing God. He used an analogy of knowing all about Edgar Martinez, his stats, and his accomplishments, his life. Yet knowing all about Edgar and knowing him personally were two vastly different things. Dean confessed that he had never met Edgar Martinez in person. He likened it to knowing about God and knowing God on a personal level. Behind the pulpit, Dean's face was red with angst, but his posture was sure. His passion quickly became infectious. His face brightened and voice animated as he delivered his new and improved sermon.

Dean dominated. His voice motivated the audience, whose eyes were bright with interest. Dean placed first in state competition, third in international competition. More importantly, he encouraged many in the wake of his passion and walked away changed himself. This was a young man transformed!

Of some thirty kids that took this class, I delighted in watching each find their own unique voice. Every student placed in the top three in state competition and the top six in international competition as they came up against talented students from six different continents and dozens of countries.

The lessons learned here can embolden all of our voices. Size, age, impediments, fears, failures, and background should never stifle your voice. Anyone with the tools to communicate can superpower their message. These tools can empower voices for the rest of their lives. I hope you, along with the students that I worked with, can continue to find a voice and the courage to deliver it. The words of a spaceship captain in the 1999 science-fiction comedy film *Galaxy Quest* say it best, "Never give up, never surrender."

Reviewing the steps these students took gives us insight into how to express our message as a powerhouse of relatability, authenticity, and depth. It is not merely about the mechanical steps of putting your voice out there. It is about enriching your voice so that it resonates in such clear and powerful tones that it becomes irresistible to the right audience.

The moral of this chapter's story is to press on. One of Disney's most endearing characters is the blue tang fish known as Dory, from *Finding Nemo*. Dory suffered from "short-term memory loss." In real terms, Dory may have had a form of amnesia known as anterograde amnesia, the inability to form or retain new memories. It was not her disability that defined her as much as her can do attitude and upbeat demeanor in the face of obvious challenges. She was endearing and inspirational. I would argue that it was her challenges that made her relatable to movie watchers and her endurance that inspired them.

Dory's friend and Nemo's father, Marlin the clownfish, sat in dismay after his son was taken from him. Dory cried out to him, "Hey Mr. Grumpy gills. When life gets you down, you know what you gotta do? Just keep swimming, just keep swimming. What do we do? We swim, swim, swim." It is reminiscent of the words of Dr. Martin Luther King Jr, "If you can't fly, then run, if you can't run, then walk, if you can't walk, then crawl, but whatever you do, you have to keep moving forward." Just keep swimming.

SECTION 2

NICHE YOUR VOICE

Lack of direction, not lack of time, is the problem. We all have twenty-four-hour days.

—Zig Ziglar. author and motivational speaker

CHAPTER 8:

THE SOUL OF A SUPERVOICE

A firm foundation

THE HUMAN SOUL is, to many, a mystery. Pixar's 2020 animated movie, *Soul*, was a charming, jazz-filled contemplation on the origins of human souls, personalities, unique quirks, and interests that make us who we are. It was a reflection on the gifts, talents, and abilities we have and how we were meant to use them to express our passions and impact the world.

In the film, Joe Gardener is a hopeful and brilliant jazz pianist who dreams of sharing his music alongside the greats. Joe trudges along as a middle school band teacher. He opines, "Music is all I think about. I was born to play. It's my reason for living."[16] Joe had found his voice, his passion in life.

Joe's life was cut short. He believed his on-stage destiny was cut short as well, before his *voice* was heard. Joe learned, through the course of the film, that his voice and story are unique but there are many ways to express passion. Your story need not be like anyone else's to be heard. There is a unique outlet for the music of your soul.

Building on your foundation and embracing your frailty, you can bring your passion into focus. To do this, you must first seek enlightenment. Enlightenment comes from our values. It is birthed from our deeply held beliefs and faith. It

---

[16] Docter, Peter, director. 2020. *Soul*. Pixar Animation Studios, Walt Disney Pictures.

is the illumination that excites and grounds us. It is vital in connecting other people to our passion.

Think of your entire being as a car carrying precious cargo, your message. Our soul is our vehicle that will drive our message onward. Enlightenment is the fuel; it is the enthusiasm that moves us to share. Our passion is the cargo that we deliver to the world. It takes all of these elements to distribute an effective message.

How do you find and focus your message? You do it by finding and focusing your passion. Passion is birthed from the song of your soul. To understand the song, you must understand the importance of your soul and what it is.

What is a soul? The soul is that priceless essence of who you are, housed in your physical shell. It is believed that we are comprised of body, soul, and spirit. This is the trichotomy theory, not unlike the concept of the Trinity, which is Father, Son, and Holy Spirit, a single God in three distinctions. You are a single person consisting of these three vital parts. The body is, of course, your physical being. It is the physical wrapper that you are packaged in. The spirit is that vitality that gives life to physical organisms. Then there is the soul. The soul is the *who* of who you are.

The soul is comprised of thought, will, and emotion. Your soul is the most authentic part of you and it is truly the most vulnerable. If you are to thrive in life, you may consider that soul expression is at the heart of your soul health. In turn, it is your soul health that gives life and passion to your expression.

It seems like a simple concept. If we want to be physically healthy, we exercise and eat well. If we wish to be spiritually healthy, we seek enlightenment. If we desire a healthy soul, we must indulge in healthy connections and expressions. We feed our individual souls with the food they most need. That in turn feeds our passion. As we feed the soul, we give richness and value to our soul's expressions. Soul enrichment comes through education, experiences, and relationships. If you are to find and express your passion, you must feed your soul.

Try to remember learning something that fascinated you, a piece of knowledge, and how you experienced, in that moment of discovery, soul enlightenment. In an interview I had with astrophysicist and Founder of Reasons to Believe, Dr. Hugh Ross, my mind was blown as he spoke about new scientific evidence for the uniqueness of our home, planet Earth. What he said exploded in my mind like a feast that enlightened my innermost being.

Way back in 1995, astronomers discovered the first planet orbiting a nuclear burning star. At that time, they predicted that we were going to find a plethora of planets, just like the planets in our solar system. Author and lay-theologian C.S. Lewis said as much in his book, *The World's Last Night: And Other Essays.* Lewis asked the questions, "How can we, without absurd arrogance, believe ourselves to have been uniquely favored?"[17] Since then, science may very well have found some contention with Lewis and the thinking of the last century.

Dr. Ross pointed out that we have now discovered a good 4,760 exo-planets, a planet that orbits a sun outside of our own solar system. We have also found that not a single one of these planets is like any of those found in our own solar system. It was shocking to hear that we have yet to find a match to any of our eight planets.[18]

There is more to this amazing discovery. Each one of the eight planets in our solar system seems to play a crucial role in making advanced life possible on planet Earth. In turn, it may, indeed, take an entire universe to support life on this one planet. Earth may be like you and me, completely and spectacularly unique. That would, indeed, make us highly favored. Thinking about it enlightens my mind. It impassions my soul.

Can you recall the last time you saw a stunning sunset and how it fed something intangible inside of you? The Big Island of Hawaii has a spectacular golden sand beach that kisses the lush shoreline near Puʻukohola Heiau, a famous temple built by King Kamehameha I in the 1700's. Kneeling off this beach, in the calm, warm Pacific, surrounded by island history, I watched as the vibrant colors of the sunset melted like butter into the vast blue ocean. It was as if I could reach out across the water and literally touch the sun as it seemed to liquify before my eyes.

Just as civil twilight unfolded and the sun gave its final bow, a sudden green flash of light took me by surprise. The green flash, a dazzling phenomenon, happens as the sun dips below the horizon. The light is dispersed through Earth's

---

[17] C.S. Lewis and Lyle W Dorsett (editor). *The Essential C.S. Lewis.* (Scribner, 1964)

[18] *MyMichelleLive Podcasts*, "Sci Tech Talk: *Unique in the universe,*" Host, Michelle Mendoza, aired September 7, 2021. http://www.mymichellelive.com.

atmosphere like a prism. Stunned by the awe and beauty, I could not move for several minutes as tears welled up in my eyes. My soul was impassioned.

From the pages of your memory, think about your most memorable kiss, a hug from a loved one, or the last time you said and meant the words, "I love you." Beyond art and enlightenment, the beauty of human interaction, friendships, and family are fundamental to the filling and impassioning of our souls.

When we do not fill our souls and effectively disperse what is in them to the world, we and the world are all the poorer for it. We all suffer. It can be a sense of restlessness or a feeling of inner turmoil. It can feel like an unfocused passion within. Our world today is rife with unfulfilled souls and broken soul connections.

Somewhere in the box of Cracker Jacks there used to be a prize. The interplay of candy-coated peanuts and popcorn was delicious to me as a child, but it was the mystery toy inside the package that excited me the most. I would take handfuls of the treat at a time, stuffing my little mouth in the process, to lighten the box and make it easier to dig deep for the treasure. Likewise, those things that invigorate your soul are a prize worth digging for. The value of that prize is in direct relation to the depth of your soul. It is birthed from experience and portrayed with the uniqueness of you.

The goal here is to excite you from the core, then fine tune and focus your enthusiasm into an effective message. Next, utilize the things that make you unique to share that passion as only you can. Use what they referred to in the movie *Soul* as personality traits, quirks, and talents, to give it life. Learn tools and techniques that make your voice more effective. Acquire skills to add to your soul's repertoire and improve your abilities. Then deliver that beautiful thing within you to a waiting people.

If communication is the voice of our soul, then, like Joe Gardener in *Soul*, we do not want to be one of the 151,000 souls that depart this earth each day before we find our passion and how we were meant to express it.

CHAPTER 9:

SUPERVOICE MOBILE

Getting direction to start your voice's engine

JUST A HOUSEWIFE. Dinner, kids, laundry, rinse, and repeat. It was her life. She had long ago set aside her dream of studying the stars. Her home was cluttered with books on astronomy, astrophysics, and star charts, all for a dream that never would be. A woman with a husband and kids in the 1960s and 70s often gave up her childhood aspirations for family. Instead, her hopes were invested in the next generation. Truly, she was much more than *just a housewife*. Yet, her engine never got running, never took her towards her ambitions, never traveled towards her intended destination.

From a young age, Mary was fascinated with what lie beyond, especially space. A bit of a bookworm, she found science journals as entertaining as novels and spent much of her time delving into both. The stars were her passion since she first gazed up at the night sky. She had hoped that maybe, when she graduated high school, she could become a research scientist, an astronomer. She could survey the universe using math and physics. She could make amazing discoveries that could, one day, make a difference.

Tulsa, Oklahoma, 1956. While walking home from school on a late summer day, science books in hand, poodle skirt swishing as she walked, Mary's life changed in a moment. An unreasonably dashing young man drove slowly by. They caught each other's eyes. His shiny red with white trimmed

1954 Chevrolet Bel Air convertible was not nearly as stunning as his smile. And what a charmer!

Mary and Pete quickly fell in love and, mere months after meeting, ran to another state to wed. Mary was only sixteen years old at the time, Pete only a few years her senior. Nine months later, their first child arrived. Nine months after that, child number two made her way to the world. Then, over a decade later, a third. Their marriage lasted nearly 50 years until Mary's death from renal cancer, three kids, and three grandchildren later.

Mary's life goals took a familiar turn towards raising her family. While she never again pursued the formal study of the stars, she infused stardom into the dreams of her children. Mary was brilliant, well-read, and taught her daughters the value in education, learning, and betterment. She put an importance on intellect, articulation, and the idea that you can do and be anything that you put your mind to. This was her legacy. This was my mother.

In today's world, a woman like my mother, Mary, would have more access, resources, and assistance than ever before in human history. With these, her story may have turned out differently. Online education, internet access, special groups, financial grants, and work from home opportunities abound in our age. No matter your situation, today there is a way for your passion, dreams, epiphanies, talent, and experience to find expression.

You may be like Mary and know what it is that drives you from a young age. What ignites your soul? What do you love to do? What is something you just cannot learn and research enough about? You may have that part of the equation figured out, but need focus on how to proceed.

Others may need more help in pinpointing their particular passion. They may be a bit more like me, where focus took a little more effort. Perhaps you are talented in special areas. Rudimentary sparks may have grown and developed. Think about what you have really gotten good at over the years. What is it that you have experienced and lived through that you can help others overcome? What is it that you have become so well versed in that you have forgotten more than most people will ever learn? These are passion sparks.

People who love us can often see those sparks more clearly than ourselves. A priceless person in my life that encouraged a spark of passion was Gussy, a beloved neighbor and surrogate grandmother. From the time I could walk, I would hold her hand and stroll barefoot through the rich dirt of her backyard garden two doors down from us. We would often go on short walks to call on neighbors. One wheelchair-bound woman, Eunice, particularly looked forward to our visits. I would sing and entertain the ladies for hours. I would write plays, complete with commercials, and solicit the neighborhood kids to play parts. We would perform on Gussy's front lawn during sunny days. God bless Gussy for sitting through every performance with enthusiasm. She encouraged my spark.

Those sparks may have emerged in your world from a young age. Gussy said I was a born entertainer. Thus, most of my interests played to my strengths. I sang in church, performed in plays on stage, played instruments, entered beauty pageants (which I hated), was a cheer leader (which I liked), spoke to groups, did walk-on rolls for television, and acted in movies.

As we mature, so do our interests and experiences, but to find our passion, we need direction. In addition to entertainment outlets, I also loved playing and watching sports, traveling, and cooking. I found writing, music, and poetry fulfilling. Archeology was crazy interesting to me. Science fascinated me. Each month, my college major would change to the chagrin of my parents. I had sparks, like a sizzling sparkler on the Fourth of July, that ignited from many things. Still, I had no direction.

You can look at someone who knows what they want to do, someone who works their whole life to do it, and be wowed. You may feel like you are missing the mark. You can wonder what your purpose is. You may ask yourself, "What am I supposed to do with my life?" I asked these questions too. My mother infused in me a confidence and along with it a belief that God does not make mistakes. There was a path for me as there is for you.

When I dug deep for my root passion, I found one thing that motivated me, that gave me purpose. It was faith. My faith brought all of my passions into focus.

Broadcasting my passion became a culmination of the things that jazzed me. My root passion melded them into one concise message. In one show, I might interview the head coach of a local major league sports team. I love sports. The next, a micro-biologist would be on my schedule. I am fascinated by science. I may talk with a music legend in one afternoon and a financial guru the next. *Boom. Boom. Boom.* One by one, each topic checked off an interest or past area of study. Yet, all of these topics and interests would be out of focus, like looking through a fuzzy camera lens at a bunch of hazy images, without a root focus. Faith was my root in every topic. I looked for a faith story, the "God story", that brought focus to my passion.

It takes a spark to start your engine. It takes special people, like Gussy and my mother, along with hard work, to fan the flames of passion. Once you tune into that spark, you can get your engine rumbling. That working engine can be dropped into the right vehicle and take your passion to the world.

Your vehicle is how you will communicate to your waiting audience. For me, broadcasting, podcasting, public speaking and performance became my career focus. This was my vehicle. The vehicle I am pulling out of my garage now is the *Find Your Voice* book and classes.

What will be your vehicle? Podcasting? Videos? Writing a book? Public speaking? Will you pursue teaching classes? *Ted Talks*? Small groups? What will you use to take your passion to the world? Wherever your destination, it is best to have focus, to know what you are doing and where you are going before you set out.

$$\bullet \ \bullet \ \bullet$$

The sun by day and moon by night. These were the tools of navigation as man first explored his surroundings. Later, sailors used sextants to find their location based on the position of the stars. Since then, mankind has used maps, charts, radio positioning, and atlases to get from here to there. Never be afraid to ask for directions, as my dad was. As many men of his time, he was never good at asking for directions.

Back in the day, before seat belt and car seat laws, some kids traveled with a virtual playroom in the back of the family station wagon. The old Ford Gran Torino station wagons, with the wood paneling down the side, had that familiar extended trunkless back. That area, behind the back seat, is where many kids would ride. Big, long windows gave us opportunity to make faces at passing vehicles and to see all the sites we passed. Toys and snacks, blankets and pillows, as well as children, rolled around, unrestrained with every turn.

This was where I was often relegated. Far up in the front of the car, my parents enjoyed a little separation, adult conversation, and music to drown out the noises of children in the back.

On a late summer trip across the state, I could hear the frustration from all the way in the front of the station wagon. My dad was lost and irritated. Mom would often send my dad and me away on summer trips so that she could enjoy peace, quiet, and a good book alone. Our car was anything but peaceful and quiet as my dad wrestled with an old paper map. Unfolded, it covered the steering wheel and most of the windshield, so much so that it shielded the view of oncoming disaster.

My dad did not notice that, in his frustration, he had crossed the center line. That is until we heard the blasting horn of a big rig. The map went flying out the driver's side window as dad swerved, overcompensated, and ended up slamming on the breaks just before hitting the side guardrail. I was flung into the back of the seat, lucky that it was soft and forgiving. All of the toys, the ice cooler, and the suitcases were not as accommodating, as they pounded into me. The next portion of our trip was a desperate search for a gas station, to ask for directions and to purchase a new map.

If only dad could have asked for directions sooner. If he had written down where to go before we left it could have been a different story. If only he had global positioning satellite assistance beamed into a convenient device, like a handheld portable phone via a downloadable map application, that story would have turned out a bit differently. Today, we tell our phone where we want to go and it gets us there.

GPS is made up of an assemblage of satellites that relay signals from Earth's surface. It can determine where your signal came from and show you where you need to go. GPS can do other amazing things that many of us never dreamed of. Did you know that GPS is now being used to monitor volcanic action and earthquakes? It can be used to analyze our atmosphere and weather. GPS can even be used to prevent shark attacks. Your cell phone, complete with GPS, can pinpoint your location to within one to ten meters. But GPS is worthless if there is no address to navigate to. All of the technology that we have in our hands cannot help us if we do not know where we want to get to.

As you start your engine towards your new venture, you will be best served with step-by-step directions. This is where clarity and focus come into play. Get in your car, start the engine, put it in gear, and press the accelerator. You are on your way! The question is, where? Where are you going? How do you get there? This is where the rubber hits the road. Here is where some of the hard work really starts.

CHAPTER 10:

LASER VISION

Steps to finding & focusing your voice

SMASH!! THE REVERBERATING sound of shattering glass from the neighbor's window sent a shockwave of terror through my spine. It froze my friends and me in mortified terror! The outdoor summer street game of baseball turned into weeks of yard work to pay off the cost of replacing the Schuler's front picture window. I was the one who threw the baseball, but we all paid the price. That afternoon, my dad took me to the park, far away from glass windows, to teach me how to play baseball, how to focus my aim.

How is your aim, the aim of your voice, your message? With a little help, you can avoid throwing in the wrong direction. You know what you are passionate about. You have dialed into what you want to share with the world, and you may have an idea of the outlet that you want to use to do it. You are well on your way to a platform for success. Now it is time to format and fine tune your message. When you have a laser-focused pinpoint to your passion, it is easy to direct it to where you want to go. Your success will be a direct result of your level of focus!

If broadcasting is your aim, you will need to learn about formatting a show. What techniques do professionals use for sharing, broadcasting, interviewing? Equipment, marketing, where and how to post; these are technical issues that may seem daunting. While important components, there is something vital that must come first.

A young athlete has a dream of playing in the big leagues. He has natural talent, a passion, and vision. He buys the equipment, suits up and starts to play the game. Without a coach, with no direction, without practice, and without sage advice from those who have played this game before, it is unlikely that he will just walk on to a major league team and get signed the next day.

Anyone can purchase equipment. Anyone can download apps. Anyone can start broadcasting, writing, speaking. They may even be lucky and, with little help or training, get to where they want to go. However, it is like buying a lottery ticket. Countless people buy tickets; someone may win. Everyone else will not. If you really want to achieve your goals, before cracking open the mic, writing your book, or teaching your class, abandon dumb luck for focus.

As you step into play, as a communicator, with a little guidance and training, you can focus your talent and passion. As is with all worthwhile endeavors, there are steps to fine tune your communication message and pinpoint your aim for connecting with an audience. Follow these steps and you will be ready for the game.

WEED THROUGH

Your level of success in communicating your message is in direct relation to your level of focus. The more focused, the more effective you will be. The most successful communicators have a focused message and purpose. To get there, you need to do a little weeding.

If you have ever started a vegetable garden, you know it is a lot of work. The thought of fresh, organic, quality produce gleaned from your own yard is thrilling. You envision such a glorious crop that you must carry the excess by the armful to share with neighbors and friends.

As your first sprouts break through the soft ground, you realize that if you are not on top of weeding, the weeds will take over. They will choke out your plants and steal the nutrients from your crop. You need to focus on your vegetable plants and not allow everything else to take over. If you do not, by the end of the season, you will be disappointed. Now you must either learn from your mistakes or allow your sad harvest yield to discourage you from trying again.

The weedy garden is like an unfocused message. You delight at the initial idea, but end up frustrated at the results. Unfocussed passion is just another weed in the garden to your audience, until you can find your niche.

Proper communication focus will result in a niche, the exact focus of your passion. This niche is more than just important, it is vital. Our world is overrun with information and those that are sharing it. Your focused message is something that others can dial in on like a GPS finds an address.

One of the biggest mistakes of communicators is having too broad a message. As a young announcer, I wanted to reach as many people as possible, so my focus was wide reaching and undefined. The result was a diluted passion. This generalized approach has the opposite of the desired effect. When people come to feast on your product, it gives them nothing distinctive to sink their teeth into.

Go to a Mexican restaurant. Order tortilla soup. If they serve up a watered down, tasteless chicken broth, you won't likely go back. If the restaurant gives the customer something like they will find anywhere else, they may or may not come back. If the restaurant's soup is delicious and bursting with flavor, it will be remembered. If it is unlike anything else in the city, people will line up to order it. When you return to the restaurant for that soup, you know exactly what you want and exactly what you will get. You'll go back again and again. Your audience is the same. Give them what they are expecting, your niche, and serve it up fabulously. They are sure to return again and again.

START BIG

Woodcarving is one of the oldest forms of art. An old man sitting in a rocking chair on a Southern porch, on a lazy summer day, wood block and blade in hand, comes to mind. He whittles down the block to make a sculpted treasure.

Passion, like a block of wood, needs to be shaved down before it reveals its most beautiful artistic result. To fine tune your message, start with your generalized ideas. Your head and heart may be brimming with ideas, passions, and plans. Write them down.

For some it is harder to identify what they are best gifted at. For help, use the "phone a friend" option. Ask those close to you what they think. Write a list of their ideas combined with a list of what you are most interested in. Then ponder how you would use this passion to help others. Once you have that specific passion in mind, whittle it down to your niche.

NICHE UP

Gem cutters study rough gemstones intently before determining what shape the final stone will take. Inclusions in the stones, orientation, and the original shape all factor into the work that will be put into its formation.

Every passion begins as a rough uncut jewel. Studying your passion and asking a few key questions will help you form your rough passion into a niche. To find your niche, ask yourself what your deepest motivation is? Who do you want to reach or help? What can you do for them? What will this do for you?

While compiling ideas for this book and *Find Your Voice* classes, I asked myself who I wanted to reach. I wanted to reach people who want to start successfully broadcasting, podcasting, and communicating their message. What can I do for them? I can use my master skills of communication and experience to help establish a message and teach the secrets of communication superpowers to make their presentation into a high-level and professional venture.

When I started my radio broadcasting career, I aired in a major city where the airwaves were jammed with options across the dial on both AM and FM frequencies. Why would someone pick my show over anyone else's? I learned the idea of niching from an older, wiser, nationally syndicated radio host. He told me that I would never taste real success until I focused my message with a specific audience in mind. "Stop trying to be someone else and do someone else's show. They are already doing it and doing it better," he said. "No one, however, can do you like you can. Fine tune your message. This is what gives your audience a sense of what to expect."

My niche in broadcasting was, "Finding the God story." Whatever story or topic that I would take on, I would ask, "If there is a God, what is He doing in all of this and what would He ask of us?" That focus brought in listeners who longed for deeper meaning, hope, or a lesson in the stories of the day. That was my niche and reason to tune in.

When I tuned in to my niche, listeners tuned in to my show. Our program took a radio station, which in its fifty years had never made a showing in the Neilson's ratings, and within months it had a top-rated show in the afternoon drive time slot.

The radio station did not suddenly and benevolently start to spend more money on promoting my show. I did not suddenly become more talented. My voice did not unexpectedly become angelic. The change came when I took the advice of someone who had walked this road before. I niched up. My product became relevant. People had a reason to find my show in the midst of the competition.

My show may not be everyone's cup of tea. Not everyone cares about finding the God story. Your endeavor will not be for everyone either. Remember that you can please some of the people all of the time, you can please all of the people some of the time, but you can't please all of the people all of the time. If you want your efforts to be successful, your best bet is to find your own niche. Do this and you will reach the audience who is most interested in that message. You can then work to please that special group all or at least most of the time.

STEPS FOR NICHING

You may be years into your mode of expression, or you may be just starting your journey. There is not a time when niching or re-niching is not extraordinarily beneficial. To find your niche, you need to dig deep to pinpoint your real, raw point of passion. Decide who you will reach with your message and how it will benefit them. Give your niche a name. Brand it into a concise and relatable entity. The natural result is clarity.

STEP 1: DIG DEEP. Looking up and down the cold, grey, misty beach at the tail-end of twilight, you could see the headlamps of hundreds of people for miles in each direction. The dark sand was still soaked and foamy from the outgoing tide of the Pacific Ocean. Under the brightening moon, people were combing the ground, looking for tell-tale bubbles rising from dimples in the sand. These "shows" revealed the underground hiding place of the coveted Pacific Razor Clam. These clams are popular for their meat and can grow to an impressive six inches in length.

Harvesting razor clams is an exercise in digging deep. Using a clam gun, which is a large PVC pipe with handles at the top, you plunge your device into the sand. Wiggling and pushing down is a race against time, as you try to get to the clam before the clam can shimmy away. You work your way through sand that is the consistency of wet cement to about two feet down. If it was not hard enough to get your clam gun down to that depth, then get ready. The real work comes in struggling against the wet suction of the sand to pull the gun up. If you are in luck, there in the muddled wet sand, pouring from your gun, is your delicious prize.

The first time I weathered the cold, dark beach to hunt down razor clams, I awoke the next morning to muscles that I had not known existed. It was a lot of fun and a lot of work. The deeper I dug, the better the result. The deeper I dug, the harder the work.

Finding your niche, likewise, is hard work. It starts with the real, raw you. This is where you do a deep, deep dig. But like digging for clams, the scrumptious plate at the end makes it all worthwhile.

Begin with that passion of yours. What is it that you want to do with it? Dial that in, then ask yourself why? For me, I had success in my career as a talk show host. I amassed extraordinary experience. I can program a show in my sleep and have helped many people launch their own communication efforts. I have made the transition to online videos, podcasting and vodcasting, writing, and public speaking, making it into a full-time business. With this book and the classes, I want to take what I know to others.

Why? Ask that question again and again of yourself until you get to your root passion. Many life coaches use this technique, encouraging their clients to ask "why?" five times or more. It takes at least that long to peel back enough layers to really unearth the root. You are looking for the real purpose that drives you. When you get to that motivational core, you will find the real part of you that will most powerfully reach the right people. Its reach is not just to any people but the people that need and want to hear that specific message.

Like meeting a smarmy salesperson who wants to close the deal at any cost, people can spot the disingenuous from a mile away. But someone who is real draws people like a magnet. It is why understanding and breaking the cycle of doubt and defeat, and using fear and failure to your advantage is so important. That real, raw you at the core of your message will be what moves the marker and makes a difference.

The "why" exercise is essential. Why do I, Michelle Mendoza, want to help people find their voice? Why? Because I have experience and knowledge and love sharing it. Why? Why do I love sharing it? Because I am grateful that I have found unusual success. Why? Why am I grateful for that success? Because my mother had unfulfilled dreams and was so happy to see mine fulfilled. That drives me. Why? Why does that drive me? Because when I look at the people who I work with, like my mom, they are living unfulfilled. Why? Why does that motivate me? Because if I help someone else, it is like I am honoring and helping her. Now we're getting down to the nitty gritty! Why? Because in helping others I am honoring, loving, and in a sense helping my mom who motivated me by believing in me!

There it is, my raw, real point, right there. I cannot help my mother fulfill her dreams; she has long passed. Yet, my love for her drives me to be that help to someone else. My mother put all her efforts into her family and into me. I am so grateful that with the support and belief of my mom and others, I made dreams happen. I want to give back to honor them and her memory.

This "why" exercise has been used by some of the most successful individuals in the world. They have learned to focus by asking the right questions. What is the real, raw point? Ask and re-ask that question. Write and re-write the answers until you really understand why you want to find and express your voice. Pinpoint your motivational root. This is part of the foundation that you will build your venture on.

STEP 2: AUDIENCE AVATAR. Your message is a perfect fit for the right recipient. The most successful messages have a specific focus and are finely tuned to communicate to a specific audience. To do this, you create the profile of the perfect recipient. Some call it your audience avatar.

If your email correspondence does not have a specific "address", it may not reach the intended destination. Try writing a letter, sticking it in an envelope, and putting on the address line, "To someone who cares." Congratulations, you have just sent a "dead letter". The Mail Recovery Center, nicknamed the "Dead Letter Office", is the U.S. Postal Service's official "lost and found", the final resting place of undeliverable mail. Craft your message to no one in particular and you will effectively have a dead letter communication.

Let's get specific. Who is it that you want to help? This is how you create the perfect recipient of your message. Since we are looking to please some of the people as much of the time as possible, who are those people? Make an avatar of your perfect recipient. What is their age, what is their life situation, how do they live? What are their needs? What are their frustrations? You can never get specific enough. Then endeavor to answer what they might want to hear from you to help, enrich, or educate them?

When you create a profile of your listener, it does more than give you that all-important focus. It helps you personalize your message. It can take your message from a broadcast to "Radioland", or a speech to "you guys", to a conversation with a single real person. You create a more loyal connection when you speak one-on-one than when you direct your message at the masses. So now that you know who you are talking to, it is time to show them who they are listening to.

STEP 3: NAME IT. Standing in the tree-filtered moonlight beneath her balcony, Romeo looks up at the girl who has captivated his soul. He longs to smell the scent of her long, soft, dark hair and taste her full, pink lips. The glance from her eyes intoxicates him. Juliet, in turn, aches within her chest, and with every breath longs to be in the arms of her love. Yet, they were enemies as well as lovers. Their families had a bitter rivalry, the Hatfields and McCoys of the Shakespearian world.

In the most famous dialogue of the play, *Romeo and Juliet*, Juliet, in longing and frustration says,

> *Tis but thy name that is my enemy;*
> *Thou art thyself, though not a Montague.*
> *What's Montague? It is nor hand, nor foot,*
> *Nor arm, nor face, nor any other part*
> *Belonging to a man. O, be some other name!*
> *What's in a name? That which we call a rose*
> *By any other name would smell as sweet.* [19]

---

[19] William Shakespeare, G Blakemore Evans et al (editors), *Romeo and Juliet. The Riverside Shakespeare*, vol. 2. (Houghton Mifflin, 1974).

So, what is in a name? Juliet only had it partially right. Who a person is, is what matters, as you foster romance between you and your betrothed. However, in the world of communication, a name is everything. Names give a sense of who you are. They are your label, your branding. Like being in a supermarket looking for soup, without a label, you stare at shiny silver can after can with no sense of how to select the right product. Without a good name, you are an unfound destination in the communication GPS.

In choosing a name, think of your audience. How will they best find you, understand who you are, and get excited about tuning in, all from your name? To help in your name quest, you might research the availability of domain names that coincide. Make sure the name is not already taken. Experts also recommend staying away from initials. In the days of telephone books, many people would use AA towing or ABC athletics to get in front of the competition alphabetically. That is no longer useful.

If you are too general, you risk losing your focused group. An overly generic name will give no first impression of who you are. If you choose a more generic name, you must work just a little harder to build your brand and define what that name means.

Try to not limit yourself in case of growth. You may start as *Bill's Mustang Talk*. Are you all about cars or horses? People will not know. Cars? What happens when later you realize that you talk about more than just Mustangs? You talk small engines for boats and motorcycles, auto repair, and more. You find that you also enjoy talking tools and equipment, but all from the perspective of a Ford Mustang lover. So instead of *Bill's Mustang Talk*, you choose the name *More than Mustangs and Motors with Bill*.

Consider running your prospective names past people who know you and your voice the best, friends, and family. Ask them for suggestions for names for your broadcast, book, or business. These suggestions can help you sift through ideas and find a name that can define your purpose. Remember that in the end, your name should be something that excites you and defines your voice.

What is truly in a name? Your parents gave you a name. It may have had significance to your family, such as being named after a favorite relative. Your name may have a definition or meaning which your parents hoped would help define you. Your given name, however, is not defined by your great, great grandparent or a definition from a baby name book. Who you have become defines what your name means to others. As you choose a name for your voice or project, that name will define a first impression in the minds of others. That impression is extremely important. As you express your voice, you give that name vital definition, fleshing out what you are really about.

STEP 4: YOUR 10 SECOND COMMERCIAL. You meet someone for the very first time. You exchange small talk about what you do and where you work. You are excited to share your new venture with them. You rattle off the name of your endeavor and then stop. Now what do you say? It could be a long litany of explanations, definitions, and chatter about your passion. As you watch their eyes glaze, you can almost hear them thinking, "How do I get out of this conversation?" Then it hits you. You wonder if this is the same effect that you will have on an audience. Hold on. Before you give up, you simply need more of that focus we were talking about. You need a concise message that your new friend can put in their communication GPS.

To laser-focus your voice, you will create a ten-second commercial. It is a commercial of who you are and what you want to do. It is an integral part of branding. A ten-second commercial is basically a spiel about you. This tool is spectacular in helping you pinpoint your focus.

My ten-second commercial would be, "I'm Michelle Mendoza, author of *Find You Voice* – a book and masterclasses. I help you focus your message and unleash your communication superpowers to share your passion with the world." It sounds like the by-line of this book for a reason. I have gone through these steps as well.

This is a technique used in network marketing to whittle down a message into a short, concise hook for sharing with others. You might consider crafting a ten-second, thirty-second, and sixty-second version. As you formulate your commercial, bring out your personality. Try not to be too dry. If you have just ten seconds to wow someone and hook them into listening to you or doing business with you, what would you say?

You are looking to hook the right audience. Thus, you have to use the right bait. It is the wide appeal versus the right appeal. If you go for the wide appeal, you might miss the right kind of audience and waste your time on a host of people who have no interest in your efforts. If you have the right appeal, you will hook the people who will love you and bring others to the table. That is a much better return for your effort.

At that very heart is your precious audience. It is all about them, not you. The one subject everyone can get excited about is themselves. They want to know what is in it for them. You are asking them to give something valuable to you, their time. What will they get in return? Your commercial will have more appeal if it is written with your recipient in mind.

To write your commercial, answer these questions. Who are you? Who are you looking to help or connect with? What can you do for them? Finally, have a call to action.

The best commercials are an outpouring of you. They meet a need. They have a good story to them. They may hit an emotion point. They entice while entering a person's world in the middle of a conversation already going on in their head. This commercial is your passion in a nutshell. So, take your time in putting it together. You will be amazed at how often you will use this commercial as you build your dream.

If you are writing a book, it may be the title and tag line. Creating a page for videos, making a web page, or starting a group gives focus so that people know exactly what you are about. If you are making your passion into a business, it helps you to get to the right customers. If you are starting a podcast, it helps to bring in the right listeners. Whatever the way of expressing your voice, you now have a concise focus and pitch.

Your commercial will also help you stay on target. You know who you are, who you help, and what you are doing. You are setting yourself up for success.

I was on a recent fishing trip. It was a glorious day with perfect weather and calm seas. Between reeling in salmon that tugged at my line, I sat playing a guitar on the bow of the little sixteen-foot motorboat. Heading home, however, our main engine would not start. The spark simply would not ignite. Our kicker, the smaller engine with a rope pull, would not turn over. The sun was getting lower over the hill. We were miles from home and dead in the water. For an hour we tinkered. We dropped anchor and sat immobilized.

Where the expression of our passion is concerned, some of us are dead in the water. Finding your voice is formulating what motivates you, how you wish to share it, and who you will share it with. It takes focus.

When finally, on my little fishing trip, the engine ignited, we celebrated. The power of focus is like the relief of turning that ignition and feeling the rumble of the engine. The spark of passion ignited. We can now head towards our destination and take our message to a waiting world.

SECTION 3

SUPERPOWER YOUR VOICE

If more people follow their superpowers - and everyone has one - then we're going to be better as a society.

—Adam Neumann, Israeli-American businessman

CHAPTER 11:

THE SUPERPOWER SECRET

Learn the communication superpowers

U P, UP, AND away! The exhilarating fictional superhero, Superman, took his first flight in the imaginations of Americans in 1938 via DC comics. The world was on the verge of war, once again, and in need of something to both believe in and to distract. Writer Jerry Siegel and artist Joe Shuster debuted the comic book hero. With enduring power, Superman has been part of the American fictional landscape ever since.

The comic presents Superman, born on the planet Krypton during a tumultuous upheaval that led to its ultimate destruction. Krypton cataclysmically explodes due to a build-up of internal pressure at its core, and all life that inhabited it is annihilated.

Superman was but an infant when he escaped the fate of his planet. His parents send him off in a rocket ship, through the void of space, where he lands on a small farm on our planet. This story was the beginning of a more than 80-year American fascination with Superman and the idea of the superhero.

Having superpowers alone does not a superhero make, though. A hero must rely on good character, good choices, good associates, good use of skills, and an understanding of his weaknesses and how to overcome them. Superman eventually joined the Justice League, partnering with other likeminded heroes. In doing so he multiplied his strengths by playing off those around him.

If we do not know what our strengths are, we cannot effectively use them. If we do not face our weaknesses, we will never get stronger. In the end, both we and the world miss out.

Your communication style is your superpower. To express your voice, you will need to learn what your powers are and begin to harness them. You will need to learn what your weaknesses are and how to overcome them. It may not be easy at first, but as Superman eventually leaned to focus, control, and use his powers, so too will you. With time, experience, trials, and tribulation, we can hone our power to use it for the betterment of all.

Watch a Superman movie about his origins and you will see that it was not always easy for the young version of the American hero. Clark Kent, his name from his adoptive parents, struggled. Finding and focusing his powers was at first awkward, if not outright dangerous.

In the 2013 *Man of Steel* movie depiction, a young terror-filled Clark, roughly ten years in age, bolts out of the classroom. X-ray vision has turned his teacher and classmates into living skeletons. The intensity of super hearing makes every noise squelch in his head. He flees past lockers, classroom doors, and down the hall to the solitude of a janitor's closet. In the dissonance of amplified noise and the sounds of the distant whispering of mocking students, he sits powerless, comforted only by a bucket and an old mop. Young Clark is immobilized and in tears until his mother makes her way to him. "The world is too big," he says to her, quivering as he speaks. His mother helps him to make his world smaller, in other words, she weeds through the noise and helps him to focus.[20] Clark Kent, before becoming Superman, had to learn about his powers and fine-tune his abilities. The finer the focus the more fabulous the success.

You, like young Clark Kent, have a golden opportunity in finding and focusing your own voice's superpower. Put an *S* on your chest and get ready to take on the world. It will be, at times, uncomfortable, awkward, frustrating, and difficult. Everything that is worthwhile in life requires hard work and struggle. Just remember that you are worth it, your voice is important, and your waiting audience is hungry for it.

---

[20] Snyder, Zack, director. 2013. *Man of Steel*. 2013. Warner Bros. Pictures.

Name any character from a superhero comic book and you will see them in your mind's eye. You will associate them with their superpower and unique gifts. The Fantastic Four, a Marvel Comics' creation, is a team created by artist Jack Kirby and editor Stan Lee. The gifts of these young heroes appear after exposure to cosmic rays. Members of the group are named for their abilities. The Invisible Woman can turn invisible. The Human Torch has the ability to generate flames. Some heroes possess multiple powers. You are gifted in at least one of the communication styles that are vital to finding and sharing your voice. Those superpowers are waiting to be focused and unleashed on the world.

WHAT ARE THE COMMUNICATION SUPERPOWERS?

Successful communication of any kind has four elements or powers. These are the voice's superpowers that draw in and keep an audience. Leave any of these out and your endeavors will fall short. Communication must be engaging, entertaining, informative, and inspirational.

Superman used X-ray vision, super strength, superior hearing, and lightning speed to accomplish his missions. We use engagement, entertainment, information, and inspiration to reach and to retain an audience. If your presentation lacks any of these elements, your task will be difficult. Information, inspiration, engagement, and entertainment are the legs of the table that make any communication stand.

Information is food for the soul. We crave it. It is vital for our growth. It gives our minds sustenance as human beings. A good broadcast, book, or lecture is nothing without bits of information that feed our hungry audience.

If information is sustenance, then engagement is the comfort food of communication. Engagement makes information taste better. It is the spoon of sugar that makes the medicine go down. Engagement creates relatability. It is what helps our message become genuine and in turn reaches our audience on a deeper level.

Entertainment is the flashy show that draws people in and can keep them attracted to our message. Food photography makes a dish look so inviting that you can almost taste it when viewing a picture. Your mouth may water just by looking at it. Entertainment is what makes our message inviting. Entertainment puts the fun in a functional presentation.

Finally, it is inspiration that spurs us on. Inspiration provides vision and motivation. It makes use of what we have acquired. Without it, we get obese and lethargic from our consumption of information, engagement, and entertainment. Much like a body takes in what we eat, it will turn our food to fat if we do not use the food as fuel. Inspiration puts what we have read or heard and turns it into something usable. Inspiration spurs us towards action.

Each of these elements are superpowers. You have at least one of these in your genetic makeup. Others you may have acquired through your life experiences. Some you may find you lack and will need to find other superpowered friends or develop your own secondary skills to supplement. When you can put all of the powers into practice you will have a winning act.

There have been scores of Hollywood actors, sports figures, and rock stars who fell flat in the communication world because they relied on their sole superstar power with no understanding of what their weaknesses were. They might be entertaining but lack the substance of information. Someone can be inspirational or informative but put their audience to sleep. You can really like someone on a personal level and feel engaged, but they may lack anything that inspires you to listen again.

Queen Latifah is an engaging actress, singer, and rapper. In both 1999 and 2013, she hosted the *Queen Latifah Show*. In both cases, it lasted less than two years. Wayne Brady is a brilliantly funny comedian who became known for his role on ABC's improv television show, *Whose Line Is It Anyway?* I saw him live at a large concert venue pick random people from the audience and with four pieces of information on their lives (name, what they do for work, marital status, what they were wearing), he sang an impromptu song about them that had the audience in stiches. Wayne Brady is entertainment personified, but his daytime talk show did not make it past two seasons. Jane Pauley, author, news reporter, and, at one time, co-host of the *Today Show*, was born to inform. *The Jane Pauley Show* came on air in 2004 and was off after one season.

You would think a sports hero would be an inspirational superhero worthy of a talk show. L.A. Laker Earvin 'Magic' Johnson had a show called *The Magic Hour;* it debuted in 1998. The show lasted only three months. Magic could not pull off the trick of balancing the sports world gift of inspiration with entertainment, engagement, or information.

If these icons of the entertainment industry cannot make it, how can the average, everyday person hope to succeed? Ah, the first thing is to recognize the fallacy in that question. There really is no one who is average. We are all unique and priceless. Our stories are important. Learn what your superpower is and how to cultivate the powers you lack, and you will do what these celebrities could not.

WHERE DOES YOUR SUPERPOWER COME FROM?

Snowflakes are renown for their uniqueness. No matter how many billions of them fall from the sky, there are never two that are the same. "In 1885, scientist Wilson Bentley devised a clever way of attaching his camera to a microscope so he could take photographs of snowflakes in greater detail than ever before. Getting this close made it even clearer that no two flakes were the same, no matter how many Mr. Bentley examined."[21] A snowflake's unique make-up is a product of temperatures, cloud conditions, humidity, and the interaction of water molecules. Like these frozen wonders of nature, we are a unique byproduct of many factors.

A person's communication superpower, strengths, and weakness are a result of an interplay of ego, experience, and environment. This is one reason that you are completely distinctive, the only one like you that has or ever will exist.

The exact relationship between these factors is uniquely yours. Ego is your temperament. It comes from a genetically pre-determined programing within you. Ego is what nature gives to you. What nurtures you is your environment. Environment is what and who you have been surrounded by. Experiences you live through will influence your personality and communication style as you react to the circumstances of life.

You may have entered the world wrapped in an ego blanket of a strong-willed personality. Your parents may have been quiet and introverted. That environment your parents supplied brought a whole new aspect to your personality.

---

[21] BBC "Why are all snowflakes unique?" Accessed September 9, 2021, https://www.bbc.co.uk/bitesize/articles/zmqmrj6.

Then you have experiences, early on, as you navigate the school yard playground. There, among the swings, kids, and slides, you developed interpersonal skills. The experiences you had there, which bring anger, pain, laughter, and enjoyment, molded your communication skills.

You exhibit a dominate superpower in the communication world that comes from your hardwired programming of ego, environment, and experience. While all the communication styles can float around in your persona, one usually drifts to the top. (You can visit www.findyourvoice.fun to take a communication style quiz that can help you pin-point that power.) You may see in yourself traits from these powers as you read on. You may also find other powers seem fairly foreign to you.

While we can pin down your dominate superpower and track some of your personality traits, quirks, and tendencies, it is impossible to put every person in a perfect personality box, wrapped with a bow, and accurately labeled. Science has tried this before, but science is intrinsically ill-suited in navigating the nuances of a person's disposition. Think about it. How do you scientifically measure character and emotion or recreate the exact circumstances that brought out their subtleties? How do you traverse an ever-changing temperament? You are in a continually fluxing state of growth and development. That is great news. That means that you are unconfined. You can grow, develop, and improve.

WHAT IS YOUR SUPERPOWER NEMESIS?

Superpowers have a flip side. They come with devastating weaknesses. Being from Krypton, Superman had superhuman abilities that others on Earth did not possess. Earth's weaker gravity and makeup of our sun gave him his strength, speed, and endurance. Yet Kryptonite debilitated Superman, rendering him powerless. Kryptonite is a fragment of the planet Krypton that, in the Superman story, emits a unique radiation that weakens Superman but is generally harmless to humans. It is interesting that being from Krypton is Superman's strength and yet Kryptonite is his weakness. So, too, our strengths have a counter side, like a coin, that can undermine our success.

Someone who is forthright and strong-willed can come off as overbearing and insensitive. Someone who is fun and fancy-free can project a disingenuous air and seem to lack substance. An intellectual may want to share their knowledge but lack the engaging superpower to keep their students interested. These are the antithetical elements of strengths.

Understanding your weaknesses will empower you. For some, it is difficult to hear the negative or take critique. Yet constructive criticism is an honest, sincere feedback that is offered to the recipient with the pure intention of helping the recipient to excel. Failure strengthens us. Without facing the adverse and its analysis, you are doomed to mediocrity.

A college professor friend of mine said that there is a big difference in generational focus at this time of his career. He noted that within this new batch of students, all members of Generation Z, many have never had a figure in academia say anything adverse to them. No teacher has ever said anything negative. This professor is a master of "sandwiching" criticism. (*Sandwiching* refers to placing a negative assessment between praise and encouragement.) He said that for some of these young students, even a gentle sandwiched critique would result in a complete meltdown. This may not be you. Criticism, nonetheless, is rarely easy for anyone to take. Those who learn to embrace constructive criticism, recognize potential faults, learn from mistakes, and work to correct them, have an edge in life and love that others do not.

Do not be intimidated by the other side of the coin! As we have discussed, your weaknesses can be your taskmaster for growth. There are ways for you to use your shortcomings for communication betterment. There are ways to build up other strengths in your life so that you can become more well-rounded, effective, and offset weaknesses. Be encouraged. Imperfections make you beautiful and relatable.

Imagine starting to play a new instrument for the first time at this stage of your life. When I picked up a guitar as an adult, my fingers ached and the ears of those around me did as well. I worked hard to build up calluses, strength, and agility. I wrote music and lyrics with the hope that I could venture out to the world to present my craft and creations. The problem was that I had a huge deficit or, more accurately put, tiny deficits! I have small hands. My poor little fingers are short for a guitarist. Bar chords are the bane of my world.

One night at Tim's Tavern during an Open Mic Night, where any one can come in, sign up, and play, an old guitarist known as "Lonely Steve" sat down with me. Steve had long silver hair and gnarled fingers. He had been playing the guitar since 1960-something. In his time, he played with big names and toured with others. Today, he often cannot remember the words to songs but still never forgets his way around the fretboard. Steve noticed that I struggled a bit. He's seen it all before. He told me that if I grappled with my left hand, bar chords, and finger stretching, then I could become more of a master with my right hand with how I pick, strum, and use creative rhythm. He praised my singing voice, expressing that that strength offsets some of what I may lack in playing. That bit of advice changed me and bolstered my hope and confidence. If you lack in one way, there is always a way to make up for it.

To overcome any weakness, you may also consider surrounding yourself with people of other communication styles and giftings to shore up what you may lack. It is like Superman forming a fellowship with other members of the Justice League, Aquaman, Wonder Woman, Batman, and others. The League's members have powers, abilities, and insight that Superman does not possess. Working with a team can enhance skill and ability. A good team will have your back.

As you read on, you can discover more about the communication styles and why they are considered superpowers. You will learn their strengths and how to focus them for effective use. We will also examine their weaknesses and get tips on overcoming them in the world of communication.

CHAPTER 12:

SUPERPOWER REVEAL

Which powers do you possess?

THE COMMUNICATION STYLES of entertainment, engagement, inspiration, and information are the elements that every broadcaster needs. Each are laid out in this chapter. Their importance, their strengths, weaknesses, and suggestions for overcoming those weaknesses are included. Additionally, there are excerpts from the quizzes that are available to the public at www.findyourvoice.fun. We can associate each communication style with a well-known fictional superhero. Understand that your gifting is, indeed, like having a supernatural ability.

As you read through the definitions and explanations of the four communication styles, note the characteristics and how important they are to expressing your voice. Think about how they might align with your own personality. Take notice of what you relate to. Write down or highlight the weaknesses that hit close to home. Think about how all of these factors affect your communication with others. The better you understand your superpowers and weaknesses, the more successful you will be at finding and sharing your voice.

THE ENTERTAINER

Entertainment is vital to communication. Without the entertainment factor, people can quickly lose interest. Entertainment helps the message come alive.

The need for entertainment comes from our social and cognitive processes, which are programmed for imagination. *Psychology Today* published a piece entitled "Why Entertainment is so Entertaining." In it, author Peter Stromberg cites Psychologist Michael Tomasello, and reference others who have suggested that we have a virtually automatic capacity of imagining what others are saying, doing, or trying to convey. This capacity is one of many things that separates us from other primates. "It is this that enables us to cooperate with others in building human culture and language."[22]

It is the expression of our imagination that reaches out to others, drawing them into our story and experiences. Entertainment is the shiny aspect of conversation that catches the eye and captivates our attention. In pre-historic times, mankind could have been crouching by an outdoor fire, telling stories of hunting mastodons. Today, we may be sitting behind a computer listening to a podcast on current events. Whatever way we receive our information, though it may have changed over the years, entertainment is key to stimulating imagination.

STRENGTHS

If you are an Entertainer, you have the golden touch; you can make any venture enticing. You are bursting with allure and appeal. Your vivaciousness can truly dazzle an audience.

You are quick on your feet, an out-of-the-box thinker. You are less likely to have to follow a script. These things make you well suited for interacting, interviewing, and monologuing.

You have a natural energy. Every opportunity is a chance to highlight something inside, dying to get out. You are not often afraid to venture into new territory with enthusiasm.

---

[22] Peter G. Stromberg, PhD., "Why is Entertainment so Entertaining?" *Psychology Today*, August 29, 2009, https://www.psychologytoday.com/us/blog/sex-drugs-and-boredom/200908/why-is-entertainment-so-entertaining.

You can fascinate yout audience with concepts others have not thought of. You illustrate points easily. You appear energetic and charming to those around you, with a naturally pleasing and charismatic persona that translates well into the entertainment realm.

WEAKNESSES

Your weakness is the flip side of your strength. As an Entertainer, you are fascinating but sometimes unfocused. You may be quick on your feet but that can lead you to step into territory you are not familiar with and have little knowledge about. When this happens, you may lose the audience's respect.

You can err on the side of flash and fancy, missing facts, and function, and can unwittingly come across as flighty and unreliable. People love to be interviewed by entertainers, as it makes for exciting dialogue, but entertainers can talk too much. You may forget the power of listening and allowing others to have their say.

SUPERHERO AVATAR

The Entertainer might relate to the Marvel Universe superhero known as Star Lord a.k.a. Peter Quill. Quill is the leader of the team known as the "Guardians of the Galaxy." He is the hybrid offspring of a human mother and god-like, alien father. Born on the planet Earth, he also spent many years among the stars. Quill's vivacious personality helps him to adjust to the harsh environment of space as he learns the tricks and trades of space rangers.

An Entertainer communicator, like Star Lord, is good at being the life of the party. He can bring pizazz to any situation. He is a natural performer, dancing his way into danger with his 1970s playlist of songs. He also has spectacular party conversation skills. The entertainer knows how to energize and make things happen.

As with all superheroes, along with strengths, Star Lord and entertainers like him have debilitating weaknesses. Star Lord has to work a bit harder to earn respect. He may be endearing but can lack emotional follow through. Star Lord is given to insecurity and can put personal satisfaction before the greater good. Nevertheless, he is an effective and enthusiastic leader.

SOLUTIONS

For Entertainers, distraction is the enemy. As you develop projects, you must have a plan for getting back on track. If you make a conscience choice to organize your time by rewarding yourself with the fun tasks only after completing the mundane, you can have even greater success.

As an entertainer, you like to push through to new frontiers but without at least a few boundaries set, you can lack direction. Boundaries, rules, and outlines will provide something for you to fall back on when you lose your way. Structure will provide reliability in relating to others.

THE ENGAGER

Engagement is the glue that holds a communication project together. It can be defined as the interaction and connection between the consumer and the communicator. Engagement is the personal and human aspect that makes a message relatable on an emotive level. It is the driving force behind the questions of, "What do you think about this?" and "How do you feel about that?" Engagement connects things and people.

Engaging an audience is vital to communication. In our world, choices seem endless. An audience is under no obligation to tune in to any broadcast or listen to any speech. They can consume whatever they choose, whenever they choose. Thus, in all the noise and impersonal communication, engagement is vital. The Engager provides authentic social interaction giving the consumer a sense of connection and loyalty.

STRENGTHS

As an Engager, you are warm and easily relatable. Your audience can feel they know and trust you in short order. This is an important part of communication. Like a faithful friend, yout audience will want to spend time with you. You will create an atmosphere of loyalty and comfort. Using creativity and insight, you can see beyond what is on the surface, reaching a deeper and more important level. Your non-verbal communication skills empower communication. Your imagination and creativity help you relate ideas to others. A picture is worth a thousand words, so to speak. You may be a natural storyteller, painting images in the minds of your audience. An Engager is gifted in bringing people together. You are extraordinarily effective in creating an engrossing message.

WEAKNESSES

The Engager's gift of connecting can work against you by causing you to attach too closely to an issue; failing to see other points of view. You can then become distracted by your passion. It can keep you from seeing the big picture. Your superhuman ability to emotively connect can cloud logic. This communication style can also be more easily swayed than the others, as an engager is gifted in identifying with others. This can make you appear wishy-washy, though.

You may find it difficult to cultivate the motivation needed to see a project through. Watch out for tasks, conversations, or presentations that can be out of focus and meander. You have a depth of caring, so dealing with constructive criticism, taken too personally, can be debilitating and can stifle your efforts.

SUPERHERO AVATAR

The Engager might relate to the superhero known as Groot. Groot is one of the most unique beings in all of the fictional cosmos. A member of the "Guardians of the Galaxy" team, he is a sentient tree-man.

Groot is strong, yet tender. Though calm and quiet in most instances, he is known to unleash his strength on any enemy foolish enough to threaten his allies. Groot's strength is beyond the physical. It is in his connections to others.

Groot is limited to three words, almost exclusively in the same order, "I am Groot." He can articulate just about anything with these limited utterings, and he has a vast non-verbal vocabulary. Groot can speak and read between the lines.

He is vulnerable to termites. Yes, it can be the little things that can bring him to his knees. He can be easily distracted by things that seem insignificant to others. While Groot is fierce, this weakness can make him unfocussed.

Tender yet mighty, gentle yet strong Groot is a walking dichotomy and a lovely creature. He has deep roots, emotional roots. These bring a budding beauty to his team.

SOLUTIONS

Engagers are gifted in connecting. To overcome weaknesses, use this gift to connect your ideas and passions with research and data. Backing up your feelings with facts gives your audience more meat than fluff. Take it a step further by connecting with counterpoints to your ideas. Understand the other side. You will develop by finding and making persuasive arguments against your most deeply held ideals. This alone can grow and deepen your message as well as your understanding of those who may wish to connect with you. Learn to engage in healthy conflict. Your empathic gifts will make debate easier for others to digest.

Bullet points are your best friend in growth, they will keep you on point. In your dreaming, write down your goals and think about the steps required to get there. Truth, honesty, and harmony are powerful allies. Always remember that information, entertainment, and inspiration can balance your approach.

THE INFORMER

Our brains are always, "on," and thus in need of continual feeding. It is a process known as neuroplasticity. It is the brain's ability to grow with new information and input. We crave it like a kid craves candy. Today we live in the information age, a historical period characterized by our thirst for information and ease of access to it. Information is what grounds any communication or project. Without it, you are left with fluff. Like a bowl of whipped cream, communication without information might look and taste good at first but it will leave the consumer unsatisfied in the end. Information titillates the mind and connects people on an intellectual level. Information is the commodity that people can walk away with that gives value in any communication effort.

STRENGTHS

If you are an Informer, you are extraordinarily well suited to fill the need for knowledge. You can be well researched and educated on issues and points of interest. You have keen powers of observation and can assess situations quickly, moving to respond with practical solutions. You are hardworking, organized, and orderly. If you have this communication style, you like to have your ducks in a row and your projects well planned out. This is immensely beneficial to your audience, who can be both educated and be given a sense of order. Steps for getting from point A to point B are presented in logical and fact-supported ways. Your communication efforts are structured and predictable.

WEAKNESSES

As an Informer, your superpower makes you reliable but not always relatable. As you share your voice, you are creating a kind of relationship between you and your audience. Facts do not a relationship make, nor a point automatically understood.

You can be perfectionists. There are few things that can halt a project's progression like perfectionism. Your own worst critic, you can see your work as never good enough. Conversely, you can overcompensate by being haughty, arrogant, and condescending. You can come off as insensitive, sometimes judgmental, and even stubborn.

You can be resistant to new ideas and get set in your ways. This can be off-putting. Reluctancy to change brings inflexibility. That inflexibility makes unfamiliar, unstructured environments paralyzing. Broadcasts and communication outlets are quite often unpredictable and are famous for presenting last-minute changes and issues. This can be stressful for anyone but especially the Informer.

SUPERHERO AVATAR

The Informer might relate to the Marvel superhero known as Mr. Fantastic, a.k.a. Reed Richards. Richards is a founding member of the Fantastic Four. He is a master of mechanical, aerospace, and electrical engineering, as well as chemistry, all levels of physics, and human and alien biology. *BusinessWeek* listed Mister Fantastic as one of the top ten most intelligent fictional characters in American comics. He is a thinker and an analyzer. Mr. Fantastic will assess a situation and quickly separate truth from misinformation.

Mr. Fantastic is flexible in body, but not in mind. He has the ability to convert the mass of his entire body into a highly malleable state, becoming incredibly stretchy, expandable, or compressed. This physical flexibility does not always extend to his mental and emotional flexibility, as laser-focus can give him a one-track mind. In this way, he is the living definition of the absent-minded professor. Mr. Fantastic can get so caught up in evaluation, examination, and extrapolation that he misses interaction and becomes incapacitated with inaction.

He can unwittingly weaken his team with judgementalism, as well as lack of emotional support and understanding. This is not to say that he does not have deep feelings and emotion. He is often harder on himself than his friends and team members. Mr. Fantastic is the go-to man for answers and will always be the friend that will tirelessly find solutions for those in need.

SOLUTIONS

Understand that your desire to be the best at what you do should include being a master in the art of growth. If you need to grow in empathy, understanding, or flexibility, then try to appreciate the process as you might appreciate the procedure of growing a sample for a science experiment. It takes time, the right environment, and observation. Remind yourself that stagnation happens from lack of change. Just because it has been done that way, does not mean it is always the best way and cannot improve.

Schedule into a continued project times for new sections, people, questions, and ideas that you may not have introduced before. Practice spontaneity. For example, in conversations or in interviews, take a moment to put down the list of questions and see where things go. Then after a little time, return to the questions to get things back on track. Your lightning quick mind may enjoy the challenge. Your naturally ordered thinking will help you to succeed over those who just "wing it".

Always try to bring something that makes you smile to the table. It can be a story or a memory that can drive your point home. That something might be a friend who can add an element of entertainment, engagement, or inspiration to your efforts. This can help you to entertain, connect, and engage your audience so that the priceless information that you are sharing is more easily heard.

THE INSPIRER

Inspiration takes us beyond our current circumstance and awakens us to new possibilities. It is not in our human design to thrive in stagnation. It is in our nature to strive, discover, and grow. Motivation Science shows us the vital importance of inspiration. "If you are motivated, you learn better and remember more of what you learned."[23] Inspiration is the communication element that gets us off the couch and moving. Without it, we fester as we feed ourselves endlessly with an overload of entertainment and information. Inspiration gives your audience something to strive for and believe in. Inspiration gets results.

STRENGTHS

If you are an Inspirer, you are a natural communicator and leader. Your communication can turn ideas into powerful words to share in any public venue. You are a superior storyteller, which is a powerful way of reaching an audience. The communications world always benefits from your charisma.

You know how to put the 'act' in activist, because of focused vision. Your altruistic and magnetic makeup motivates others to believe that they too can change the world. No matter the passion, it is easy for you to spur others on.

You can often see the potential in those around you that others miss. This passion is motivational to others. People may love to be entertained, informed,

[23] American Psychological Association, *"Psychological Science Agenda: June 2018,"* Accessed September 7, 2021 https://www.apa.org/science/about/psa/2018/06

and engaged, but it is you that is the force that moves the audience beyond consumer to producer.

Challenge to you is an opportunity to push forward. When focused, you identify the objective, execute the plan, and readily welcome any trials that arise. You are a force to be reckoned with.

WEAKNESSES

Energizing and enchanting, but not always endearing, your message can get lost in your method. The same magnetic personality that draws people in can actually repel when perceived as stubborn and overbearing. You may be a good listener, but you have a strong sense of how things should be. This can generate reactions which are perceived as judgmental, condescending, or irritating.

The enthusiasm behind your passions can limit them at times. It can make it difficult to see when you are wrong. You can forget that it is in vulnerability that our greatest ability to connect and inspire lies. At times, passion drives you to charge heart first into a situation before thinking it through. You will leap before looking.

You have a tendency towards overcommitting as you are driven to help and fix any problem that arises. Your vision can be unrealistic and overly idealistic. That over-the-top passion is what inspires your audience, but without balance it can, just as quickly, turn them away.

SUPERHERO AVATAR

The Inspirer might relate to the DC Comic's superhero known as Aquaman, aka Arthur Curry. Arthur Curry is the son of an Atlantean princess and Tom Curry, a lighthouse keeper in Amnesty Bay, Maine. Curry grew up on the shore but eventually left the lighthouse life, venturing into the oceans, to live out his true destiny as King of the Sea. This amphibious superhero is adaptable, adventurous, and assertive.

Aquaman, as the product of land and sea, became the bridge between these two worlds. Aquaman had a unique skill of talking to sea creatures, humans, and Atlanteans alike. As a natural motivator, this is an ideal ability. However, he struggled to understand his opposers. It is an impressive attribute of the Inspirer, the ability to communicate with just about anyone, but it is difficult to utilize this skill if you fail to empathize with the other side.

Aquaman's strengths come from his ability to survive Earth's and the sea's greatest depths of pressure and temperature. It is a byproduct of his deep-sea heritage. Auquaman thrives in tenuous situations. He, like all Inspirers, is whom people turn to when the pressure is on.

At times, Arthur Curry does not know his own strength or how to best utilize it. He can be a bull shark in an underwater China shop. He benefits from the prodding of those close to him to learn how to focus and rein himself in.

His greatest weakness, according to DC legend, is dehydration. Like all Inspirers, Aquaman can expend so much energy that he forgets to replenish. A true superhero, Aquaman uses all the elements at his disposal to solve problems and make things happen.

SOLUTIONS

Remind yourself to focus on the moment. Dreams, commitments, and future aspirations are part of your strength, but those strengths can get quickly diluted and limit your powers if they have no foundational focus to build upon. You can overcome weakness as you learn to appreciate and master what you are doing right now and understand why you are doing it.

The tasks at hand will be best broken down into small conquerable portions. Surround yourself with people who can help you to focus and to rein you in when needed. Do not let yourself overcommit or overpromise. Do not devote yourself to tight schedules. Rather, create more fluid tasks and fewer inflexible ones for greater success.

The truth is your ally. In your desire to change the world, remember to listen. Try to understand opposition, differing views, and what motivates them. As you communicate, be mindful of logical fallacies, which are easy to fall back on in the moment, but show lack of understanding and true powerful reasoning in the end.

Think back to your best first date. If you sat across the table from someone informative but boring, interesting yet hard to connect with, or emotionally engaging but unreliable, you may not have gone back for a second date. Communication is a relationship between you and your audience. As with all great relationships there must be elements of the intellectual, emotional, inspirational, and enjoyable. The elements of entertainment, engagement, information, and inspiration must be unleashed in this communication relationship to reach and retain your audience.

CHAPTER 13:

SUPERPOWER RECIPE FOR SUCCESS

Why we need all the communication superpowers to succeed

L ET ME TAKE you to my favorite restaurant. It sits atop a city hill, overlooking a water view that is nothing short of breath taking. Your senses are enchanted by majestic mountains, backdropping the sparkling sea. A crisp white ferry boat meanders in the distance. It is easy to get lost in the final rays of warm sunlight, as the ferry waltzes a fond farewell upon the stage of the dark green waters and you indulge in your evening meal. White clothed tables, soft candlelight, and cozy booths are positioned for conversation and a bit of privacy. The smells of roasting meats in this downtown Brazilian Rodizio restaurant are intoxicating. Fresh baked cheese bread called Pao de Queijo entice you with every breath. Soft bossa nova music accompanies your rum caipirinha drink. You sip to the rhythm of the song.

The stage is set, then it is time for the main event. The players come out. Young, strapping Brazilian men parade large fire roasted skewers of meats to each table. It is as though you are transported, in your imagination, to the exotic country of Brazil. Your taste buds excite when staff slice off delectable morsels of meat for their guests.

The manager greets each patron as though they were an old friend, just to make sure everyone is having a magnificent encounter. The venue is perfect, and the food delicious and satisfying. The music and presentation are sensational, and the staff spurs you on to enjoy it all. No wonder I love the Grill from Ipanema.

A spectacular restaurant experience is like the interplay of communication superpowers. The venue is engaging. The food is inspiring. The music and presentation are entertaining. The staff is informative. This is an example of how these important elements have a symbiotic effect, creating a perfect experience at a restaurant. It can also create a dynamic experience for your audience. If one of these components were absent from my restaurant experience, the evening might turn out okay but it would most definitely not be the same. In a world of competition, every advantage can give you the edge. Put these communication elements together and *bam*! You have a recipe for success

A dear friend of mine, Darol, was the expert and talent behind a popular radio show. We lived in the same swanky apartment building in a downtown metropolis. From his near top floor apartment, you could sit in an armchair and watch NFL teams play football games in the stadium below. We met on a chilly October game night where we chatted about sports, life, and radio.

I found out that Darol hosted a weekend radio show on a top-rated station. His show was what we call in the radio business a 'pay-to-play' program. These are shows in which people, companies, or organizations pay stations to broadcast. In contrast, I was paid by my station to be on the air as a host. Pay-to-play is a form of infomercial, where clients exchange money for airtime to present their goods, services, or messages. You will hear everything from doctors to deacons to decorators in these programs. They are most often informative, but since anyone with cash in hand can buy the time, the shows can be lacking in the entertainment factor. Presenters can sound unprofessional and unengaging. These shows usually rely on selling enough product, or getting enough donations, to stay on the air. Stations pack them into time slots on the weekends when there are fewer listeners. It is a great way for radio stations to meet their bottom line, and for businesses to get their word out.

You just kind of know, or you should know, when your show is a bit lackluster. The majority of the pay-to-play hosts understand that they are not professional broadcasters. Juggling breaks, calls, and information is not as easy as it sounds. Most recognize this and will have someone from the station assist in hosting, taking calls, and getting in and out of commercial breaks. That is what you do especially if you are lacking in the essential elements or superpowers of communication. You add elements that can infuse the things that you don't have. This is one way to overcome weaknesses; get a professional to help!

There are some really, really good pay-to-play shows and hosts. But, I admit, as a professional host working at the top of my game, I wondered if my new friend, Darol, would be one of them. Sorry Darol! That is until I listened to his show. Darol had it going on. He had a good voice, strong presence, great sense of humor, and he dazzled his listeners. He had all of the elements of communication strengths working in his episodes. His show was informative, engaging, entertaining, and inspiring. Pretty much every show was like a great dining experience. You came away satisfied. Even in dealing with the subject matter that was not for everyone, "estate planning", it was a show anyone could enjoy.

Many people, like Darol, either already come with a pretty good balance of communication elements or have, through life experience and environment, developed them. Professional broadcasters have to learn quickly how to perfect these elements if they wish to make it in the business. Others, like Darol's compatriots in pay-to-play broadcasting, know their own craft but lack in the communications arena. They have some superpower but want for the other powers needed to do the job. Because Darol cultivated all of the elements, he could take on a subject matter that was vitally important, but virtually dry as desert plain, and make it into a show worth listening to.

How did my friend make a winning radio show out of a dry topic? Darol was not a professional radio host. Yet, he got it right because he applied the superpowers. He invited guests and guest hosts that could empower him even more. He thrives with personal connection, so he brought people on to connect with. Darol did one other vital thing. He knew his audience and knew them well.

Remember how we created the profile of the ideal listener? You should know their interests, music tastes, what makes them laugh, and what makes them cry. Darol did. He understood what they were moved by, got excited at, and were afraid of. He could offer just the right information and help, then inspire listeners to make positive changes. He could reach them on a deep and meaningful level, and have them laughing at the ironies of life. They felt like he got them, because he did. He used the elements of communication to engage, entertain, inform, and inspire.

Conversely, I had worked once with a big-name host who bombed on radio. While building my own radio career, I produced a few radio shows. One show, in particular, highlighted the lesson of communication strengths and weaknesses. The show's host was a well-known fitness, nutritionist, and motivational speaker. She had a brash speaking style, was aggressive in her mannerisms, and was quite inspirational. She was a self-described in-your-face, radical, feminist fitness guru. This icon of health was pleasant and motivational as she interacted with me. She was, however, abusive and demeaning to my male co-workers. A disdain for men was evident in her show as well.

This host was absolutely inspirational, that was her superpower! She was 100 percent full speed ahead, all of the time, drilling her power message with fervor. She cut down opposing views with the swift sword of her forceful opinion and pounded out ideas like a drill sergeant at the first week of boot camp. This encouraged listeners to make changes in their lives, but it was hard for them to connect and engage. Her disdain for men and unyielding ideology did not lend to an entertaining show. It did not help her ratings either. After only a few months, I walked into work to find that the show had been cancelled and the host long gone.

There was, however, an indelible lesson I took away from this experience. It hit home in the last few weeks of the show with a bizarre incident. The host bragged daily about being all natural, all organic, all green, and how she worked off her mom bod by her extraordinary will power and all natural methods. She let women know that if they were fat and flabby, as a mom, "shame on you". It was revealed, however, that she did not nurse her newborn child. That was shocking. People called in asking why a preacher of all-natural health would shirk this opportunity to nurse her son. She shot callers out of the water, "None of your (expletive) business," she quipped on air. She told her staff that it was because she had had surgical implants and fillers to enhance her appearance. After all she was a celebrity. WOW! So much for all nature all the time! This host dug her feet in the ground and disingenuously pounded out a message that was contrary to her own actions and mantra.

On the last day of broadcasting, just after the show ended for the day, this tough, brassy woman spoke with a new mom and cancer survivor off of the air. It was then that something fascinating happened. She got honest, real, humble, and engaging. She confessed to the caller that she had always had a poor body image. It was no secret that she went from fat mom to fitness queen, but after her last child, her breasts shrank and sagged. It was harder to get into shape than it was years before with her other children. She feared being judged by the world who looked to her for inspiration. It was her decision to balance plastic surgery with her proven methods of health. This was the big secret. She could not breast feed because she had implants that prevented milk production. She feared what her audience would think and say.

It was such a powerfully engaging conversation that we, her staff, stood listening in awe. If only she could have been that genuine and engaging on the air. She could have shared a struggle that was so relatable. If she knew her audience and that their struggles were not that different from her own, she could have mesmerized them. If she could have poured out the person that she was on that phone call to her greater listening audience, perhaps she could have continued to use the medium of radio to make a difference.

This situation taught me that honesty matters, vulnerability is powerful, and that the mistakes that we make connect us with others, making us relatable. If you can pull out the honest, real, raw you with the power of communication through engagement, entertainment, information, and inspiration, you can change the world. The elements that you need for communicating are vital and must be genuine. This is the recipe for your voice's success. Use it and you will gain and retain your audience.

Check out any online restaurant review and you will see that trust is easy to lose and hard to reclaim. Even great restaurants have bad days. You too will have bad days as you share your voice. You will inevitably serve up something your guests will not like. That is okay, it is part of the human experience. Be honest about it to your audience. Share your struggles, make things right. If you are willing to listen to constructive criticism, face and shore up your weakness, and use bad reviews as a catalyst for change, you can better yourself and serve your audience excellence.

A group of friends and I spent a Labor Day weekend in wine country. It could not have been a more favorable weekend. The clear skies and warm sun enhanced the joy of gathering with good friends. After a few tastes of reds and whites, we were looking forward to lunch.

A highly recommended restaurant was nestled in a vintner's village between swanky winery tasting rooms. This bistro boasted a gorgeous outdoor garden of edibles with charming walking paths. There was something romantic about their outdoor seating area, canopied by leafy white oak trees.

Our enthusiasm waned with some less than idealistic happenings. Our group of eight was separated to opposite sides of the garden. Disappointment grew as part of our group was served quickly and the other, that sat forty feet away, still hadn't gotten menus. The young staff argued with each other within earshot of customers. A woman with a wheelchair was turned away because she could not navigate the rocky outdoor ground, though there was a paved patio and empty tables just off to the side that seemed as though they could accommodate her. They told her, "This may not be the restaurant for you." One busser haphazardly sprayed disinfectant while cleaning; it wafted onto the food of the neighboring tables. Staff rolled their eyes when the patrons complained. The food was fabulous, the setting picturesque, but these faux paus dampened our dining experience.

Days like these can be a learning opportunity for businesses as well as communicators. Be mindful to employ the elements that make a consumer's investment of time and money worth the while. If you infuse your efforts with known elements of success, you are more likely to succeed.

In previous chapters, we laid the groundwork of success by highlighting the importance of your voice and how to focus it. (This is who I am, what I want to do, the real why I want to do it, and who I want to share my voice with.) All the natural talent and developed skill you can muster cannot replace this foundation. Adding the communication superpowers to your focused voice is the *it* factor that sets you apart.

With so many competing voices in every medium, these secret weapons will attract and keep the right audience. Dazzle them with entertainment and feed them with brilliant information. Keep them engaged with a sincere authentic connection and inspire them to action.

Think of utilizing your voice like a professional baseball pitcher perfects his skill. Remember that no one wakes up one day, out of the blue, embosses their name on a jersey, and shows up unannounced on the field, expecting to start in the game. Before you earn your place on the roster, you first had to recognize your love for the game, your passion. You practiced. You made mistakes and corrected yourself. You learned secrets to perfect your game as you gained tips on how to stand, aim, and use your arm. These secrets are like the entertainment, engagement, information, and inspiration and they will bring your message into the big leagues.

Your audience is your catcher, you need to focus your aim to get your message in to their hands and hearts. On the mound, you must wind up and aim your throw with laser focus, superpowers employed, to hit the right catcher in the right spot. Like sports figures cultivates their talents and employ proven techniques, so too can your voice hit your target when you learn how to use communication strengths.

Do you realize what is entailed in getting a ball from a baseball pitcher to the catcher? According to *SPORTFANFOCUS*, "Pitchers will use change in velocity (from pitch to pitch) to keep the hitter off balance and they will use late movement on pitches to miss the barrel of a bat. Every pitcher is different and will have his own combination of pitches." "An effective "two-seam" fastball is considered to be one of the nastiest pitches in Major League Baseball. It can carry extreme velocity (up to ninety-five mph) but also have late arm-side movement. A combination of elite velocity, like ninety-five mph, and late movement, make it very difficult for batters to square-up and drive."[24] It is not as simple as throw it out there and hope someone catches it.

If you bring this kind of purposeful precision to your own game of communication, you have a better chance at hitting your mark. Who exactly is it who you want to catch your message? Knowing your audience is that next vital step. It directs your message to the right receiver. Throwing that ball requires you to know your superpower strengths and abilities and how to use them. It requires you to understand and develop past your weaknesses. When

---

[24] Sports Fan Focus, "Baseball Pitches (Explained, Illustrated, and How Pros Use Them)" Accessed September 11, 2021, https://sportsfanfocus.com/baseball-pitches/> [Accessed 11 September 2021.

the game is on you have a focused message and direct aim, you are ready to bring out the heat!

Thirty major league baseball teams hit the diamond each spring. As fall edges out the warm memories of summer, only two teams remain to face off in the World Series. Both teams are talented, hardworking, motivated. So, what is it that can put one over the top? Sometimes you see it. The *it* factor. Something pulls a team together. It can turn the underdog into the top dog. I have seen it in every sport and in the game of life. I believe it comes from training, cultivating passion, developing superpowers, and digging deep into your purpose. That is the deep magic.

When a patron walks in ready to spend, a restaurant that gives the most bang for the customer's buck will be the restaurant people will return to again and again. A great manager will strive to make every guest's visit a brilliant return on his patron's time and money. He enhances his patron's experience by providing excellent service, food, and a feeling of satisfaction. An athlete who wants to win the gold medal will give his best at every event. A communicator who wants to gain and retain an audience will strive to dish up excellence at every opportunity.

Make no mistake, even if no cash changes hands, those who will listen in, watch, or read what you are sharing will be giving you something of extreme value. It is something that they can never get back and something you should regard as priceless. It is their time. Never take that time for granted. They have invested their time in you. Appreciating their precious time can drive you to the kind of excellence that your voice and audience deserve. If you give your fans a fantastic return on their investment of time, they are sure to make you a favorite destination and give glowing reviews to their friends as I do for my favorite restaurant.

CHAPTER 14:

SUPERPOWER TRAINING

Boot camp for your super voice

HARDWOOD PEWS IN long rows, unpadded, unyielding and, to a five-year-old seated there for a couple of hours every Sunday, almost inhumane. We were surrounded by stained glass and straight-laced silent spectators whose only sign of life was the occasional, "Amen." Oh, and the need to squiggle and squeal? It was nearly unquenchable. Despite an animated fire and brimstone message coming from the Baptist pulpit at our neighborhood church, I remained unengaged and uncomfortable.

If you have undergone this Sunday morning church ritual as a child, you may remember the ways that you tried to pass the time. People watching, noting who fell asleep during the sermon and who did not, were favorites of mine. Counting notes in the hymn book or doodling with little pencils on bulletins tucked in the back of pews were part of my church experience. I would watch the clock's seconds tick by, awaiting the moment the preacher said his final amen, and I was free to play out the rest of the weekend unrestrained.

I would come home from church with pink pinch marks on my leg, as battle scars from my father's fruitless struggle to keep a hyper younger version of myself under control. It is challenging enough for me to sit still as an adult, I cannot imagine my dad's frustration back then. Yet, every Sunday we went and every Sunday I squirmed, in what seemed to be a useless weekly exercise in futility.

Looking back, I would not change it for the world. Somewhere along the path of life, I realized that the wisdom and grounding from those seemingly ignored sermons planted themselves firmly in the depths of my psyche and my heart. These treasures would pop out of my mouth when I was in need of profound words for friends in need or during life's battles. They would act as road signs in guiding my life choices. Like seeds in a garden that had fallen on what looked to be dead unfertile ground, with the right nurturing, somehow, something blossomed. From all those years, I somehow heard and later heeded the positive messages laid out and began to do things in my world that reflected it.

You are here to cultivate your skills, to share your voice. To do that, you too will need to hear and then heed, and finally, do. Hear, heed, do. Like the wisdom of my youth seeded in my soul, by hearing and heeding, I came to the place where doing was just natural.

Your superpower is seeded in you and may already be blooming in your life. From there we will cultivate a spectacular harvest of communication. Your talent can blossom and be enhanced. You can sow other powers into your life, like sowing seeds in a field that will flower in your voice's garden. This is where you are encouraged to put in some work. This is where you develop what you already have and enhance it by building up areas that you are weak in. Then we can take that fortified you and create a platform to share your voice.

If you have ever heard of companion planting, you may know that it is a science of agriculture. You seed crops of differing plants near each other for pest control, pollination, and protection. It is a mutually beneficial cooperative of vegetation. For example, one type of vegetable will provide shaded protection for its companions below it. In exchange, the neighboring plant may have a natural repellent that deters insects that would otherwise plague its larger friend. Take a favorite companion duo of tomato and basil. This couple dose not just taste great together in a spicy Italian dish. In a garden, basil repels pests and worms that feed on tomatoes. Tomatoes help basil to grow and to taste better. Likewise, our superpowers need companions if we are to flourish. Entertainment, engagement, inspiration, and information are companions that flourish best when planted together.

Here you will learn how to plant the companion superpowers into your life. With a little work they can take root in your efforts. You do this by hearing, which is much like sowing a good seed. Heeding is like cultivating a growing plant. Then harvest your talents by doing!

This is where you engage in superhero training camp. Build up your weaknesses and focus your strengths. Utilize the exercises and recommendations that follow. These come from years of experience and application. They are my secret go-to ingredients in an ever-growing process of effectively sharing my own voice.

What you will see here are ways to build each of the four superpowers. Utilize them even if you know that you are gifted in an area. In fact, utilize them especially if you know you are gifted in an area. The goal is superpower ability to make you the best that you can be.

THE ENTERTAINER

Elements of entertainment in any presentation will help your audience pay attention, want to stay tuned in, and return for more. Here are some suggestions for training in entertainment.

EXERCISES

Read to Children

Children's books are rife with interesting characters and attention-grabbing material meant to keep even the most restless child engaged. If you do not have children, borrow some; moms and dads would likely welcome the break. Read to nieces and nephews via video link. Volunteer to read at a library or children's wing of a hospital.

To keep children from squiggling in their seats like kids on a pew on Sunday morning, you will need to use different voices, pitch, volume, dynamics, and inflection. Utilize pacing by reading quicker and slower, add a dramatic pause. Put emotion in emotive words. Sound sad when a character is sad. Laugh and smile as you read something that is funny. Let your face and body tell the story as well. Watch for boredom. If a child tunes out, you need to turn up the efforts to entertain.

Remember that when talking to adults, you will not employ the over-the-top antics of children's book reading but dialed down, the same tactics can be used. In this exercise, you will have developed the skills that, when implemented, infuse an entertaining element into your communication.

Tell Jokes and Stories to Grown-Ups

We have all sat around a table with friends, catching up on life and revealing stories. Sometimes stories captivate and other times you wonder, "Where is this going? What's the point?" Stories are the bread and butter of verbal communication! Not everyone is good at storytelling. The author of a book on effective storytelling gives us hope. "We are programmed through our evolutionary biology to be both consumers and creators of story…It certainly can be taught and learned."[25]

Practice by mindfully telling stories to friends. Utilize some of the aspects you might employ in reading to children. Make your voice and mannerisms interesting. Stay away from too many details! Try starting with a hook. "Let me tell you something scary that blew my mind this week." "I saw a dog do the funniest thing yesterday." "If you hate driving listen to what happened on Interstate Five today." Use visual description and paint a picture in their minds.

You might also learn from other's successes and failures. When in a gathering, take note of what stories grabbed attention and why. Remember what stories fell flat. Employ what you've garnered into purposeful communication.

Play Games

Acting games are fun and fabulous for growth as an entertainer. They train you in off-the-cuff, improvisational skills. You can play these improv games with friends and family or join an acting/improv class. Acting games can be something as well known as the old game of charades. You can look up improvisation or acting games in books or on the internet. These games provide an endless list of fun ways to liven up a party and build your entertainment value.

---

[25] John Sachs, "Winning the Story Wars: Why Those Who Tell - and Live - the Best Stories Will Rule the Future," (Boston, Mass.: Harvard Business Review Press, 2013)

Use M.A.S. Or the 'LIKES'

When in conversation, practice using M.A.S. (metaphors, analogies, and similes). M.A.S takes information and makes it relatable and visual for your audience. Where you might say, "I went to the game Tuesday, my team won. I'm glad." Instead, use a metaphor (a figure of speech in which you attribute non-literal attributes to an object). You might say, "At the game Tuesday, my happy balloon exploded when my team won!" Use a simile (a figure of speech that compares one thing to another, painting a picture of what something is like). "Tuesday, at the game, my joy level was a nuclear explosion, my team won." Or try an analogy (a comparison by way of explanation). "I was at the game and my team winning was like being a bear at an all you can eat picnic. I could not get enough." These tools help paint a picture and add an entertainment factor to your story.

THE ENGAGER

Engagement with your audience creates loyalty. It entices them to connect with you and to connect you with others. Here are ways to build the engagement factor.

EXERCISES

Put Others First

Practice doing nothing out of selfish ambition. Effective humility can poke fun at oneself, without self-deprecation. Being quick to recognize your faults or mistakes and just as quick to rush in with an apology is endearing.

You can learn to make people a priority with sincere compliments. Looking for the good in others helps you to appreciate and connect with others. Writing something or saying something nice provides instant engagement.

On social media, I had a recurring post that read, "To combat the negativity on social media, I wanted to take time to show how much I appreciate my friend (name)…" I would choose a friend and write about three sentences praising their character and what they mean to me. While for many it "made their day", it helped me to grow in appreciation, character, and engagement.

Keep a Gratitude Journal

Gratitude, according to the Aspen Brain Institute, "…improves interpersonal relationships both at home and work." "Couple studies have also indicated that partners, who expressed their thankfulness to each other, could sustain their relationships with mutual trust, loyalty, and had long-lasting, happy relationships."[26] Gratitude helps us stay engaged. Daily logging a few things that you are grateful for will help you grow interpersonally and as a human being.

Practice Active Listening

Active listening is a way of hearing others in a way that keeps you engaged. It is listening purposefully when someone else is talking. Active listening helps you to receive the gift of information that you are being given.

Here is an exercise that will develop active listening skills. Repeat back what someone has just said to you. Add phrases that can clarify what you are hearing. "What I'm hearing you say is…." Do this without judgement, advice, or your own opinion. Active listening makes others feel valued, heard, and connected with you. They are much more apt to listening to you in return.

The *You* Factor

Always, always speak to your ideal listener. It is a pin-point focus that gets one centered on the one person that matters. It is not me, it's *YOU*. It might be said that you are engaging and changing the world one person at a time. Start with the *you*, that is your listener avatar. While broadcasting, I never talk to the masses, to Radioland, or to *you guys*. I always speak to my audience as that one ideal listener, *YOU*.

---

[26] The Aspen Brain Institute, "Giving Thanks: How Gratitude Affects the Brain," Accessed November 5, 2022, https://aspenbraininstitute.org/blog-posts/gratitudeandthebrain.

THE INFORMER

People crave information! Putting out good information is like giving a juicy treat to a playful puppy. They see the treat and they suddenly focus in. Researchers at UC Berkeley's Haas School of Business found that we desire information like we desire money and wealth. These researchers have found that, "…information acts on the brain's dopamine-producing a reward system in the same way as money or food…To the brain, information is its own reward, above and beyond whether it's useful,"[27] Well-ordered communication gives good information in a well thought out way.

EXERCISES

Play Brain Games
Brain games come in many packages, from solving number problems, as in Sudoku, a logic-based number puzzle, to board games like Scrabble. Doing crossword puzzles, playing solitaire, or doing a jigsaw puzzle can help strengthen your brain's ability to analyze and distribute information. Vascular neurologist Dr. Oana Dumitrascu is the assistant professor of Neurology at Cedars Sinai. She says, "Repetitive activities and staying in your comfort zone will not improve your neuroplasticity. You need to challenge yourself every day." "Challenging your brain to learn something new—such as a foreign language or a musical instrument—has been shown, both in healthy individuals and patients dealing with mild cognitive impairment, to improve brain structures and neuroplasticity."[28] Brain games exercise your brain like a muscle and help you to better focus and sort through daily information.

Learn the Art of Debate
Many of us have a propensity for arguing but can we finesse an intelligent debate? Consider growing in the art of dialogue and conversation. If you have

---

[27] Ming Hsu and Kenji Kobayashi, "Common neural code for reward and information value," PNAS, June 11, 2019, https://www.pnas.org/doi/10.1073/pnas.1820145116
[28] Kyle Beswick, "Do Brain Games Help Brain Health?" Cedars-Sinai, September 23, 2019, https://www.cedars-sinai.org/blog/brain-games.html.

never had the privilege of debate team training, you might research how to make an effective argument and the many logical fallacies that dismantle efficient dialogue on your own.

Logical fallacies are statements made from patterns of reasoning that are flawed. They are easy to break down, misleading, and frequently spin the truth. Fallacies are often made by people who feel passionately about an issue but negate the thinking process and information gathering steps when addressing ideas. Debate helps you to organize and to back up your thoughts with logic, facts, and proper reasoning.

Be a Pattern Person

Informers are masters at gathering information and often in drawing connections. Seeing common threads in stories, how things can be similar, and finding shared ideas builds patterns that you can pass on to your audience.

Follow patterns of conversations. Create a map, in your head of how friends went from talking about their favorite band in high school to why it is bad luck to walk under a ladder. What linked those ideas together? This kind of mental investigation can help you boost the informer inside.

Play Detective

Careers in Government lays out the personality traits of a successful homicide detective. They must be curious, observant, insightful, able to draw conclusions, logical, systematic, and strong in reasoning skills. They are organized and efficient. They do not let anything fall through the cracks. They are practical and realistic but results oriented. They have high ethical standards.[29] Sounds like the DNA of an Informer!

How do you become a detective? Investigate. When you walk into a new environment, take note of where things are, who is there, how things interact. When meeting someone for the first-time, purposefully remember their name, areas of interest, and what might set them apart from others. Walk away. Do you remember what they were wearing, drinking, or the color of their hair?

---

[29] Scott Blaufeax, "How to Become a Homicide Detective" Careers in Government, September 5, 2015, https://www.careersingovernment.com/tools/gov-talk/about-gov/education/how-to-become-a-homicide-detective/

THE INSPIRER

Inspiration in communication is what changes people's lives. We were programmed with a need to become something greater, to reach beyond, and to look for new possibilities. Inspiration takes us from limitation to transformation. When we inspire our audience, there is a euphoric response that changes them simply because you spoke.

EXERCISES

Set Examples
Out of shape? What to make more money? Tired of how your home looks? Is your relationship getting boring? FIX IT! Lead from the front. Learn from others, figure it out yourself, either way, be a doer. Then share your story, your testimony. You know the struggle. You understand the pain. You can help someone through their own challenges. This gives purpose to your imperfections. How do you overcome and deal with them? That is inspiration.

Be Brave
Try new things. A young friend of mine is a powerhouse. He speaks, he travels, he is doing start-ups, he is becoming quite successful. But this young man in his late twenties admitted to me that he spent his life shy and overlooked. What changed? My friend said that he started doing anything he could that was uncomfortable. He had a bad singing voice, so he went out and sung his crackly-voiced heart out at karaoke. He would volunteer to do presentations at work. He would go up to a stranger and say hello. If he felt the twinge of, "Ugh, I can't do that," he would find a way to do it. He started off, as he acknowledged, "Sucking at everything." He became better at most things, some he has nearly mastered (not karaoke). One thing he has become is confident and, in that confidence, he is most definitely inspirational.

Be an Encourager

Learn to lift others up. Many have mastered put downs. Many do it to feel better about themselves. In the end, it has the opposite effect. Find ways to speak truth beyond someone's situation. You can become part of their solution instead of part of their problem. Simply recognizing a bad situation does nothing but point out the obvious. Rolling your sleeves up and making a difference changes the world! You can do this by searching for people's strengths and not obsessing on their, or your own, weaknesses.

A starting point is a smile. You can encourage others with that simple act of approval. Make eye contact and smile.

Do Something Amazing

Doing something amazing can be a huge inspiration, but it can be done in small unnoticed ways. Helping a mom who is juggling a half-dozen bags of groceries and two toddlers to the car is a small miracle to that mother. Saying please and thank you, or I appreciate you, is one of those small, amazing things that lightens hearts. Volunteer. Host a neighborhood barbeque. Do you see in these examples an investment in others? We are at our most amazing when making a difference. As you make a difference, you learn what inspiration really means.

Communication styles are enhanced by all of the elements of your unique and wonderful personality. Becoming a more well-rounded human by these enhancements will magnify your voice. Like a musician plugging into an amplifier, the music may be wonderful, but plugged in, it can catch the ear of so many more people. Enhancement through your superpowers is the megaphone to communication.

The side effect of growing these areas of your world is the enrichment it gives you as a person. You were created to be a masterpiece, a magnum opus. The more you grow, the more beautiful you are as a wonderful piece of human art.

SECTION 4

PLATFORM YOUR VOICE

If you want people to listen, you have to have a platform to speak from, and that is excellence in what you do.

—William Grosvenor Pollard,
American physicist and Episcopal priest

CHAPTER 15:

SHOWCASE YOUR SUPERPOWER

Creating a platform for your voice

"ALL THE WORLD'S a stage, and all the men and women merely players…" This is one of the most famous of Shakespearian phrases. It begins a monologue from the pastoral comedy, *As You Like It*, by William Shakespeare. The lines were expressed by a contemplative character, "The melancholy Jaques". He was an overtly observant, exiled nobleman, living amongst the English forests of Arden. Jaques made this perceptive parallel of life and the stage. Life is like a play performed on the stage and people are like the actors. He opines, "They (all) have their exits and their entrances; and one man in his time plays many parts."[30]

Let that linger in your mind for a moment, oh, the parts that we have all played. We enter this world, then we play out our lives as though we were celebrities in our own reality show. Throughout the episodes, we have many life experiences and adventures.

A man can be brought to life's stage as an innocent swaddled infant. He can next play the unruly child, riding his BMX look-alike bike and tossing a foam football with his friends. His next role in the play of life might be as a rebellious teenager, rolling his eyes at his parents and playing video

---

[30] William Shakespeare, *As You Like It, Pastoral Comedy*, (First Folio, 1623) Act II Scene VII, Line 139.

games in his poster-plastered room. He can later play the lovesick young man proposing to a girl at a table at their favorite restaurant. Next, he might play a husband, a father, an employee, homeowner, then grandfather. He has minor roles in this drama as a football enthusiast, fisherman, and little league coach. As an actor in your own story, you too play many parts and have many dimensions to your passion. Learning to consolidate all that you are into a professionally packaged message can help you become a star in your next roll as a communicator.

The word I hear from most people starting a new communication venture is "lost." You might wonder where to start. How do you format your message? The most powerful messages that will absolutely reach and impact your audience will be formed by following a simple recipe.

As the expression goes, "It's as easy as pie." A pie crust is surprisingly easy to make from scratch and requires very few ingredients. Four simple components can make a crust for any type of pie from banana cream to chicken pot pie. The basic ingredients are flour, salt, shortening, and water. Put together in the right order, under the right circumstances, and with a little work, you will have a flawless flakey crust.

Every communicated message requires four ingredients to make a perfect message for your voice. The most effective messages are made from a hook, a story, a lesson, and an ask. Use these elements in the right order, under the right circumstances, with a little work, add a little superpower, and you will have a message fit for any platform.

HOOK

A hook is what draws a person in. It meets your audience in a conversation that they are already having in their head or heart. You are tapping into something that they care about and promising them that their concern or interest will be addressed. Your hook is like a marquee above a theater that is marketing exactly what an audience might find if they were to buy a ticket. That advertisement is never boring. It is aimed at enticing and exciting the right crowd. Likewise, your hook draws interest and should excite the right audience.

STORY

Then there is the story. Stories are how humans have always communicated. Before newspapers and cinemas, stories were told in tribes and in families chronicling current events and historical tales.

Stories have many tentacles that reach out to pull us in, in countless important ways. They hold elements of truth, facts, history, fascination, and hope. They can touch us emotionally and intellectually. Stories can reach us with logic and with imagination all at the same time. We have an empathic ability to relate aspects of stories to our own thoughts and feelings. We can see ourselves in the characters. We can learn from their struggles.

I cannot over-emphasize the extraordinary power of the story! In an article entitled "Stories Matter: Why Stories Are Important to Our Lives and Culture", Tom Corson-Knowles, author, and founder of TCK Publishing, lists reasons why stories matter. "They are universal. Stories help us learn how to act wisely. Stories help shape our perspective of the world. Stories help us understand other people and their perspectives. Stories pass down knowledge and morals."[31] A story gives meaning to your message. It makes it relatable and interesting. It is a narrative of someone's experience. It is an illustration connecting your hook to your topic and your topic to your lesson and ask.

Bring out your life stories as related to your hook. Utilize the stories of others. Give analogies and paint pictures that make your message come to life. The story is vital to your efforts.

LESSON

In the end, your story has a point. That is what we call the lesson. It is the *ah ha* moment of your talk. The magic to stories is the moral. Every song, every comic strip, every book, and every article has a lesson. These lessons are products of yours or your audience's observations of the story. You impact your audience by helping them to see this lesson and how they can become enriched by it.

---

[31] Tom Corson-Knowles, "Stories Matter: Why Stories Are Important to Our Lives and Culture," TCK Publishing, Accessed September 28, 2021, https://www. tckpublishing.com/stories-matter.

ASK

Oxford Dictionaries defines *call to action* as, "an exhortation or stimulus to do something in order to achieve an aim or deal with a problem: 'He ended his speech with a call to action'."[32]

Your call to action is your ask. The ask moves your audience from interest to action. It gives solutions and hope. The ask changes your audience from hearer to doer. This powerful end to your message gives your followers stakes in the game. It can be used to change and enhance their world. It can be powerful for building your efforts as well.

You made a promise in your hook. You delivered it in your story. You showed them how you delivered it in your lesson. Your ask entreats them to do something about it.

There is a consistent pattern in powerful messages. All good messages, like stories, really do hold to this format of hook, story, lesson, and ask. You may have seen countless films of boy meets girl, boy loses girl, boy finds girl. The same pattern is in girl meets horse, girl loses horse, girl finds horse. Patterns are part of every message.

A professor of literature and author, Joseph Campbell had a theory back in the mid-1980s. He was fascinated with comparative mythology and religion. He poured through the history of humanity through stories, researching similarities. After deep diving into myths told from around the globe, he concluded that all compelling tales have a universal pattern. It is what he called the monomyth. In his book, *The Hero with a Thousand Faces*, he claims that stories may have different characters, settings, and cultures. They may come from different eras and geographical locations, but from Shakespeare to George Lucas, the "hero's journey" is the same.

Beyond the "beginning, middle, and end" of a story, there is what can be broken down into the following pattern. It starts with the journey of a protagonist living in their normal world. Something happens and the hero must answer the call or deal with a problem. They go into action and face a main obstacle. They defeat it and return changed.

---

[32] Oxford University Press, "call to action," Accessed September 28, 2021, https://languages.oup.com.

We can see that same basic pattern in a hook, story, lesson, and ask. In our hook we are meeting someone in that place where something has shaken their normal world. It may be concern, fascination, or curiosity. There they are searching for solutions, information, and help. We share a story or stories that relate to that need and then take them on an adventure with us. We highlight obstacles and issues and reveal how to meet them head on. In that is our lesson. We conclude with an ask, a way to return to a happier state that can benefit them and others.

My favorite movie of all time is another Shakespearian romp, *Much Ado About Nothing*. It is a 1993 romantic comedy directed by the brilliant actor, director, producer, and screenwriter Kenneth Branagh. Branagh has a gift for bringing the sometimes cryptic and antiquated language of Shakespeare to life. This little gem of a film was shot on location in Greve in Chianti and Florence in Tuscany, Italy. It boasts actors like Denzel Washington, Keanu Reeves, Emma Thompson, Michael Keaton, and other A-listers. *Much Ado About Nothing*, is a screen adaptation of a story of young lovers who will soon wed, verbally jousting rivals who are secretly in love, and a contemptuous villain who wants to spoil it all. Like all good stories or messages, it follows a recipe, it has a beginning, a middle and an end. It has a hook, story, lesson, and ask as well.

Set on a lush early summer's day on the hills just beyond the vineyards, the film has us joining in a picnic. The lovely Beatrice sits dangling her dirty bare feet idly from a tree branch, eating grapes, and reading to her friends and family as they indulge in cheeses, wine, and sweeping vistas. She reads, "Sigh no more ladies, sigh no more. Men were deceivers ever. One foot at sea and one on shore, to one thing constant never. Then sigh not so but let them go, and be ye blithe and bonnie, converting all your sounds of woe into hey nonny, nonny."[33] That is the hook. It is the sixteenth century equivalent of an ageless cry. Men suck, love stinks, ladies. So, forget about them! Let's just go have a party and sing, "Girls Just Wanna Have Fun." That is the hook. It sets the stage for a romantic frolic and jealous shenanigans.

The story progresses, as men return from war. They have come home to celebrate and procreate with marriage and mayhem. A villainous character

---

[33] Branagh, Kenneth, director. 1993. *Much Ado About Nothing*. The Samuel Goldwyn Company (United States),

sabotages the pending nuptials of the main young lovers. This results in the death of an innocent girl as she succumbs to crushing accusations of debauchery. But, alas, she is not dead! It was but a ploy to await her proven innocence and to demonstrate to her betrothed his great sin in doubting her. In the end the bad guy is found out, the wedding takes place.

In the end, true love conquers all. That is the lesson. As the final scene ends in dance and celebration, the company sings the same words that began the film. The call to action comes as they say to all who watch to convert, "… all your sounds of woe into hey nonny, nonny!"[34] There it is, the film works, the formula works.

What is your favorite film? Can you see the distinct beginning, middle, and end? Can you follow the "hero's journey'? Can you define the hook, story, lesson, ask? As you find and express your voice, it will be best heard with this secret but simple recipe.

You have a message and now you have a formula for focusing and sharing it. It is not certain to whom this sarcastic quip is attributed, but someone turned the famous quote of Shakespeare's on its ear by saying, "If all the world's a stage, I need better lighting." Put your message in the hook, story, lesson, and ask formula. Take that winning recipe, find the right stage, and you will be ready to light it up!

---

[34] Ibid.

CHAPTER 16:

SUPER VOICE DANCE

Outlining the step to success

TIKI TORCHES ILLUMINATE the sandy terrain. The shoreline pounds out a steady rhythm, and the scent of plumeria drifts on the warm tropical breeze. An amber sun sets on a Hawaiian luau.

A luau is a cultural party celebrating Polynesian tradition. It is complete with pit-roasted kalua pig, seafood dishes such as poke, and purple poi, which to many a foreigner tastes like wallpaper paste. Nearly every major hotel in Hawaii boasts luau celebrations. Haulis, or non-natives, with Aloha shirts and white zinc oxide smeared noses flock to this experience.

A hula lesson, for visitors to a luau, is a crowd favorite. Novices flap their arms and shake their torsos in unskilled jubilation to ukulele music and the pounding drum beat of a hollowed gourd called an *ipu heke*. You may get called up on stage to do a dance-off with a Tahitian-style hula dancer. Their grassed *pareo*-skirted hips rotate at high velocity. Imitating hula at a luau is fun, but true hula is a very preciously guarded cultural dance developed to retain the stories and history of the Islands. A true understanding of the ancient art of hula goes far beyond the fun portrayed with coconut bras, flower leis, and hapless shimmies. A *kumu* of hula has what might be considered a PhD equivalent of the craft and of Polynesian history. Dancers can trace the lineage of their kumu to masters from the beginning days of the dance. I was trained in traditional flat-footed hula by Kumu Noelani of Hula Halau O Na Mele O Hawaii.

Hula and communications have a parallel theme. Many people will listen to a broadcast and, like an eager tourist at a luau wanting to shake it to Don Ho's "Tiny Bubbles", they will choose to jump in and give it a go. There is a sense of excitement and fun to that. As they say, "imitation is the sincerest form of flattery". They will quickly learn, however, that there is more to broadcasting, speaking, interviews, and effective communication, just as there is much more to the art of hula. To be a master takes skill, teaching, practice, and time.

The professional sounding communicator, like the highly trained dancer, can make their craft look natural. A very good friend of mine confessed to me once that he thought that I was lazy. He would listen to my broadcast and it sounded, to him, as though I simply show up, turn on the microphone, and have a blast for a couple of hours. I talk to fascinating people. I opine on subject matters that fascinate me. I may be entertaining on air but, in the end, I collect a paycheck for just having fun. That was his impression until we worked together. It was then that he witnessed the behind-the-scenes care that is put into every communication effort. There is planning, formatting, research, and schedules. Every word and every tone are part of the mastery of communication on air. In the end, my friend confessed that my hapless, happy sounding broadcast requires precision. "You are one of the hardest working people I know," he conceded.

The lesson here is to dance like no one is watching but perform like it really matters. Express your voice. Be willing, however, to learn, train, and work towards excellence. You and your audience deserve nothing less. By learning the nuances of your chosen communication outlet, you keep yourself from looking like a novice tourist on stage. Transform your efforts into a professional sounding quality production that you can be truly proud of. It will draw an audience every time and can be worthy of pride, growth, and even monetization. Learning from Kumus of communication, so to speak, will grant you a connection to their knowledge, gleaned from a lifetime of experience and the lineage of teachers who infused their own expertise into their work.

If you were a dancer, you would learn the choreography of your dance. Choreography is a sequence of steps, movements, and motion. In communication, creating an outline is the equivalent. You create steps that make your efforts come to life. You may be writing a blog, giving a speech, doing an interview, or starting a podcast. Having an outline gives you structure and provides a map to get you where you want to go.

The basic outline of every effort is the basic outline of any message, the ever-reliable hook, story, lesson, and ask. Adding an introduction and conclusion to this formula creates a skeleton for your communication projects to be fleshed out upon. What each of these elements looks like, sounds like, and plays out to makes your broadcast as unique as you.

Broadcasters must have an outline to choreograph their program, lest it be unfocused. Speakers with no outline can find their audience losing interest as they wander through their presentation. If you are being interviewed, an outline is a pitch that will entice producers to your message. Outlines provide clarity and focus to the steps of your communication choreography. With it, your audience is more likely to enjoy your dance.

INTRODUCTION

First impressions are vital. Your introduction is the primary step in our outline. It sets the mood for what is to follow. Your introduction is a culmination of what the audience first sees, hears, and feels. It should draw them in to the experience of the message that will follow.

If you were broadcasting your own talk show, a grand introduction might begin with music, lights, sound effects, graphics, and an announcer heralding your program. A true introduction is much more than all of that. Introductions tell your audience who you are and what to expect. Your words, your attire, and your backdrop set the stage. Is this high-level professional? Is it casual and fun? Are you presenting yourself as relatable?

Your introduction must catch your audience's attention. This is where they meet and connect with you and get a taste of what your broadcast or conversation will be about. Show your audience your unique energy and give them something to whet their appetite. Never, ever let your intro be dull, boring, or dry. You have an important message, and it deserves a vibrant start.

HOOK

We have discussed how your hook offers your audience something they want or need that you promise to deliver. In an outline, it should be whittled down to a simple sentence or very short paragraph as part of your introduction. A hook can be a simple formula, "If you are struggling with this then you need to hear how I can help. An effective hook captivates your audience by making the message about them, not you. This is a specific contract you make with your audience, giving them insight into what they are about to experience.

STORY

"If history were taught in the form of stories, it would never be forgotten," said Rudyard Kipling, Author of The Jungle Book.[35] If your voice is expressed in story, your audience will not easily forget. A story segment of your outline is an illustration that you will later use to highlight your moral, conclusion, or lesson.

Nuzzled between your hook and the lesson in your outline, your story may be a first, second, or third-person account. It may be recited in news stories or played in sound and video clips. Your story may include a dialogue or interviews. It may simply be a telling of your own experience. Stories are vital to creating interest, driving home your lesson, and building engagement.

One of America's greatest storytellers was broadcasting legend Paul Harvey. Harvey took the news stories of the day and seamlessly interwove them with history, people, and commentary. He spun them together like a master wordsmith into *Paul Harvey News* and *The Rest of the Story*. He was carried on 1,200 radio stations, three hundred newspapers, and nearly four hundred American Forces Network stations. His fame centered around his ability to flow from news to tales and then to talk in flawless storytelling form.

Upon Harvey's death in 2009, the *New York Times* posted an obituary written by Robert D. McFadden. It gives a fitting description of what a true storyteller does. "[He] personalized the radio news with his ... opinions but laced them with his own trademarks: a hypnotic timbre, extended pauses for

---

[35] Rudyard Kipling, *The Collected Works of Rudyard Kipling*, (Garden City, NY: Doubleday, Doran & Co., 1941)

effect, heart-warming tales of average Americans and folksy observations that evoked the heartland, family values and the old-fashioned plain talk one heard around the dinner table on Sunday."[36] Harvey used every superpower element to infuse life, through storytelling, into every broadcast.

Your outline will not be complete without the story, something that brings life to the points, opinions, information, and inspiration that you are doling out. In each program, decide what the main point is and how best to highlight it with a story.

If you are being interviewed, have at least three short stories at the ready. Keep in mind that interviews work best in sound bites and opining should be kept to sound bites fewer than ninety-seconds. Line up good stories to illustrate important points. Employ all of the superpowers of communication to bring your stories to life.

If you are a broadcaster, decide who will be the storyteller. Will you pull a tale and illustration out of a guest, a news report, a sound bite, or from your own experience?

LESSON

The lesson portion of your outline is a statement, a conclusion. It is a moral to the story, the "ah ha" moment. The lesson connects the dots of your story and gives your audience what they were assured of in your hook. Your hook tells them what you are going to do for them. Your story does it for them. Your lesson tells them how you delivered as promised.

ASK

The ask is both a call to action for your audience and a funnel to drive your audience to an act that can benefit you. Now that you have gifted your listener with your message, the ask gives them a way to put the experience into action. You can offer suggestions for your audience to find additional information, or how they might engage deeper.

---

[36] Robert D. McFadden, "Paul Harvey, Homespun Radio Voice of Middle America, Is Dead at 90," *The New York Times*. March 2, 2009.

The ask should benefit you. This is where you can suggest that your audience buy your book, become a subscriber, join your mailing list, listen to your next broadcast, donate, or become a partner to support the efforts.

When someone has invested in you with their time, giving them a call to action is like a payoff on their investment. It gives them stake in the game. The ask is the inspiration that can make changes in their world.

OUT

Giving your ask and moving to your program's conclusion is your "out". Your out can be as simple as a "Thank you for listening." It can be music, an announcer, or you can tease upcoming programs. It should be a way of ending your program and thanking your audience for its time. This is a perfect place to employ branding, like your logo or tag line.

If you explore basic dance moves for Salsa or the Two-Step, you might find instructions with footprints, arrows, and dotted lines painting out a step-by-step framework on the dance floor for each move. Get that outline down, put the steps in the right order, and when the music starts, you will be ready to move to it. When accompanied by music and choreography, culture, sometimes a partner, and maybe props, it becomes a fascination for dancer and audience alike. In his book, *Why We Dance: A Philosophy of Bodily Becoming*, Kimerer L. Lamothe says, "Dance is movement…and every bodily movement that happens appears as a pattern that unfolds in time and space. There is no dance without a pattern."[37]

Dance is a fitting analogy for communication. Both are expression in a pure form. The dance of your voice, with the pattern of your outline, will be an expression worth tapping the foot to.

---

[37] Kimerer LaMothe, *Why We Dance*. (New York: Columbia University Press, 2015), 4.

CHAPTER 17:

YOUR SUPERPOWER HQ

Building a stage for your voice

H E IS CONSIDERED by some as the best and most decorated basketball player of all time. Michael Jordan's accomplishments in the sport include six National Basketball Association (NBA) championships, and subsequently, six NBA Finals Most Valuable Player (MVP) awards. He holds the records, in the NBA, for career regular season scoring and playoff scoring. Jordan also starred on the United States "Dream Team", in the Barcelona Summer Olympics of 1992. To say that Michael Jordan is a gifted athlete would be an understatement.

Jordan traded his basketball for a bat and glove in 1994 when he joined the Chicago White Sox AA minor league team, the Birmingham Barons. As a pro baseballer, Jordan batted an impressive .202 with three home runs and thirty stolen bases. Then he returned to the NBA and racked up a few more titles.

If that is not impressive enough, Jordan is a fairly remarkable golfer. It is said that he bet legendary golfer Tiger Woods that he would break 92 at the 2009 *Golf Digest* U.S. Open Challenge. That is a pretty gutsy wager. The thing is, he won the bet!

Michael Jordan has been seen on the big screen. He owns many businesses and he has many successful ventures in addition to playing a variety of sports. You could say he has a lot of stages to act on.

We all carry within us a myriad of talents, interests, and passions. We are a cornucopia of abilities, activities, and skills. Like Michael Jordan, we may find ourselves in differing roles at differing times of our lives and in careers that pull on those abilities. Some of these roles we master and others we give our best shot, yet do not quite make the basket. Theses outlets are the stages that we stand upon for a time in our lives and from where we share our voices. Choosing the right stage, at the right time, for our voice will help your message to be better received.

Michael Jordan may be built for basketball. He may be well suited for baseball and be a celebrated amateur golfer, but he may not have excelled at ice hockey or rugby. He is well versed in sports talk, but he is another victim of the "I think I should have a talk show, but I'm not cut out for it" dilemma. (Jordan had a short-lived talk show local to Chicago called, *Michael Jordan Airwaves*. It did not last long). Jordan succeeded where he did because he chose the best paths for his abilities. He failed when he picked the wrong paths for his powers. Picking the right stage is everything.

One of the most beautiful makeshift stages was under the blue Caribbean skies. White sands and turquoise sea were a perfect backdrop. On a trip with a group of friends, I sat at a beachfront deck with my blue travel guitar in hand. We met Miguel and Alex. Language was only a slight barrier, but music bridged the gap. Miguel and I traded the stage, performing songs in our own native languages. It was an impromptu performance. Like any of us who find ourselves sharing our voice, being prepared, focused, and practiced means that I am ready to use my voice when the stage is set.

From public speaking to beach side performances, there are endless outlets for you to share the passion of your voice. Which focused message will you be ready to share? Broadcasting, podcasting, speaking, teaching, writing, or other communications provide a stage. These stages have many platforms to play upon. As you read on, decide which venue or venues you will choose to take your voice to a waiting world.

Remember, the more focused, the more you will succeed. Narrowing the efforts of your stage is key. Where you choose to express your voice will be your vehicle to take your voice to the world. Like choosing a sports car, a work truck, an SUV, or a fuel saver, your broadcast choice should be determined by the job you want done and the vehicle style that is right for you.

Vehicles, for example, can have three basic types. They are land, sea, or air. Broken down further, you have vehicles for work, pleasure, or personal use. A personal land vehicle might be a minivan, economy vehicle, or sports car, among others. In your communication efforts, choosing the precise vehicle or platform is easiest if you understand who you are, what you are trying to accomplish, and who you want to reach.

There are three basic types of vehicles and there are three basic types of communication platforms. These are topical, ideological, and experience based. They are the three overarching areas of a broadcast or communications productions. This is the ground floor of your efforts. It is a first step in giving your communication efforts a foundation.

TOPICAL OR INFORMATION BASED COMMUNICATIONS

Information-based communication efforts can also be referred to as topic-based communications. This type of broadcast is for those highly focused on an issue or topic. It may be your passion or area of expertise. If, for example, you want to talk about antique autos, climate science, soccer, or women's health, this format is for you.

A topic-based broadcast benefits from the most detailed of niches. It is not just health, but women's health. It is not just women's health but women's reproductive health. You might specify your focus further to cover reproductive health for women of childbearing years. This sort of emphasis drives your conversations, your elements, and to whom you are broadcasting to. The more focused the topic, the more successful the information-based endeavor.

IDEOLOGICAL BASED COMMUNICATIONS

An ideological or idea-based communication focuses on a belief, perspective, or idea that is held in high regard to yourself and your audience. You and your target market may be strong believers in animal rights or you may have a faith-based philosophy. You may wish to cover health, but your passion lies in naturopathic remedies and treatments. This category is for those who may have a strong drive or belief in a political ideology. An ideological communicator has an enthusiasm for, or loyalty to, a segment of the population or group who is like-minded.

Liken it to groups that you might find on social media. Group titles and categories can be the basis for ideologically-based broadcasts. When the group is assembled due to a common belief, they are an ideological assembly.

EXPERIENCE BASED COMMUNICATIONS

Experience based communication efforts gather a following of people with a shared background or reality. Like ideological based broadcasts, the experience-based audience forms a group. They have an experience in common but do not necessarily have a shared belief. Rather, they are united because they share something similar in the happenstance of life. A mom's group that shares anecdotes and craft ideas for toddlers, homeschooling parents, men over the age of fifty, survivors of cancer; these are experience-based groups. The members may differ in politics, religion, and other fundamental ideological leanings, but they are brought together because of common life events.

These base focuses of your communication are foundational. Build on that foundation a format for your voice. What will your topical, ideological, or experience-based work look like? How will it start to flesh out? According to a senior lecturer and head of the Department of Mass Communication at Alex Ekwueme Federal University, Ngozi Eje Uduma, "…broadcasts will all fall under one of these categories of entertainment, education, talk, news or children's programs."[38]

Then build a little more. Will I give lectures, do a podcast, or preach in churches? Choosing the best category for your voice is the next step in building your stage. These efforts clear the fog, so to speak.

In the beautiful Cascade Mountains, I spent an afternoon snow skiing. I was on a run that was a bit advanced for me. Standing trepidatiously at the top of a steep, icy ridge, the weather took a sudden change. Fog and heavy snow descended, turning clear stunning vistas into a frosty veil. I was unfamiliar

---

[38] A. Duyile, *Broadcast News Reporting and Programming*. (Akure: Endurance Prints & Publishers, 2005)

with the terrain and then, suddenly, I had nearly no visibility. I felt a tightness in my chest, as my hands clinched my poles. A bit of panic set in. I had no idea which way to go. Accompanied by an expert level skier who knew the mountain well, I had a coach to encourage me in the right direction. He reminded me that the same fundamentals of the sport apply in any weather condition. He coached me down the run. As we descended the mountain, I began to sink beneath the cloud layer. The crisp blue skies opened to a stunning and welcomed panorama. I knew exactly where I was going and how to get there. That sense of knowing is the relief that we all experience when the fog lifts and your direction is clear.

Your foundation is laid. Your stage is under construction. What do you want your life's work to look like? What will be the emphasis of your efforts? What do you want to be known for? There are many famous theater houses in the world. Each have stages that boast performances from some of the most talented and renowned artists in the world. Differing theaters are known for particular crafts, styles, or genres.

The National Noh Theatre in Tokyo, Japan is constructed from four hundred-year-old cypress trees. Its name, Noh, means *skill* or *talent*. The theater is known for spectacular presentations of traditional Japanese musical drama and plays.

Shakespeare's Globe is an iconic structure. It was rebuilt in 1997 to near exact specifications of its 1613 glory after a fire destroyed the original structure. This historic theater can be counted on to present Shakespearian productions.

The Palais Garnier is in Paris, France. In 1896, its stunning six-ton chandelier plummeted from the ceiling, killing an audience member. The incident inspired a famous scene in Gaston Leroux's novel, *The Phantom of the Opera*. It is still known for grand staircases and an exquisite stage that exhibits operas and ballets.

Think of your passion staged in its own showcase. As the Grand Ol' Opry is famous for country music and Grauman's Chinese Theater, in Hollywood, is known for films, so your platform should be tailor made to house your voice.

Building on your foundation and fine-tuning your focus, you will start to see your dream take shape. Once you decide on a topical, ideological, or experiential message, you then proceed, step by step, in building your platform.

Will it be an entertainment, education, talk, news, or children's program? Will you broadcast, podcast, write, speak, or preach? As you better understand the plethora of talents, interests, and abilities housed inside of you, your focus will guide you, culminating into a beautiful edifice that platforms your voice.

CHAPTER 18:

USING YOUR SUPER VOICE

The art of public speaking

WHERE, JUST THREE days prior, a basketball game played out before a booming crowd of fans, I stood surrounded by thousands of participants in a much bigger game. It was my first state political convention. National figures and movers and shakers graced the stage of the massive arena. Booths adorned in red, white, and blue decor were hawking bumper stickers and T-shirts. They were butted up against tables peddling policy, positions, and political candidates. Lined up in row upon row, they sprawled in this seemingly endless field of faces. Standing alone, I took it all in.

A hand on my shoulder and a familiar voice jarred me out of my contemplation. John was his name. He and his wife were two of the most beautiful people I have ever met. They were passionate and brimming with integrity. What a delight to see them participate in political affairs, where some of these traits can be wanting. John shared his desire to be a delegate. Delegates are chosen to represent their state party at the national nomination of the President of the United States. A delegate is officially nominated by an attending individual and then elected by vote. I told John that I would be delighted if he would allow me to be the one to officially nominate him before the gathering.

For what seemed to be an eternity, I waited for my time to speak. People walked to the podium, threw out a name for nomination and a few nice words, to a seemingly inattentive audience of thousands. From the speakers, you could feel the angst, like a massive wave emanating from their nervous words, as they stood there before so many peering eyes. Their voices quivering and timid, they looked down at the paper held in their hands to anchor themselves, stated their business, and left the stage quickly thereafter. One woman, I recall, held the podium so tightly that she broke off a piece of its wooden frame.

It has been reported that at least 75 percent of humans fall victim to some sort of angst when speaking in front of people, at one time or another. It can range from slight jitters, perhaps nervousness, to full-on panic. Some might call it stage fright. In fact, the fear of public speaking is the most common of human anxieties; it is said to outrank even the fear of death. In its full-on phobic mode, it is known as glossophobia. Increased blood pressure, dry mouth, a sensation of tongue swelling, body heat and perspiration, muscle stiffening, even nausea are what many suffer. Though three in four people will experience some level of public speaking apprehension, it need not prevent the effective sharing of their voice.

Mark Twain once said, "There are only two types of speakers in the world, the nervous and the liars." As I approached center stage of the convention, I felt like a tiny speck, on a massive stage, in an immense stadium, before the largest gathering of people I had ever experienced. Of the tens of thousands in attendance, there could not have been more than a handful of people truly listening. Most had zoned out long before I trekked up to the microphone to speak. Determined that my efforts would not go unnoticed, I employed all that I knew of the art of public speaking. What happened next was astounding.

Taking a cleansing breath, and with every ounce of confidence I could muster, I took a moment. Then I smiled. In my best, "on-air voice", I started slow and low, building in enthusiasm. "Ladies and gentlemen, can I have your attention please?! (Pause) I am Michelle Mendoza, and I am about to share with you a nomination that will inspire your hope in America!" To my astonishment, my confidence hushed the arena. I surprised myself by continuing to speak when I wanted to stop and just shake my head, "seriously?!" As I went on to share the virtues of my nominee, I could see people in the stands hushing others as they strained to listen. With sincerity and certainty, I gave my brief spiel to the raucous applause of the gathering. Many others crossed that stage, both before and after me. Their nominations may have been just as worthy and integrous as my friend John, but they were without the enthusiastic response that my short speech garnered. Ineffective communication skills and anxiety in public speaking dampened their efficacy.

Is there a difference between jumping out of the path of a speeding car and speaking in front of a group of people? *Psychology Today* reported that, "Surveys about our fears commonly show ...Our fear of standing up in front of a group and talking is so great that we fear it more than death."[39] More than death?! Public speaking or deadly threat, you may be surprised to know that your brain often cannot tell the difference between these two scenarios. "The fight or flight response activates complex bodily changes to protect us... We need to respond without debating whether to jump out of the way of on oncoming car while in an intersection...The threat area of the brain can't distinguish between these threats."[40] Comedian Jerry Seinfeld put it this way, "More people are terrified of making a speech than dying. That means most people at a funeral would rather be in the coffin than giving the eulogy."

Fear and lack of public speaking skill leads to ineffective communication which has profound consequences. Would you like to lose 10 percent of your monthly wages? How would you like your chances of promotion being diminished by 15 percent? These are the results of a lackluster presentation. Additionally, 96 percent of people believe that communication in their daily businesses needs improvement. According to Salesforce, a customer relationship management platform, 86 percent of employees and executives blame workplace

---

[39] Glenn Croston Ph.D., "The Thing We Fear More Than Death." Psychology Today, Nov. 29, 2012. https://www.psychologytoday.com/us/blog/the-real-story-risk/201211/the-thing-we-fear-more-death.
[40] Montopoli, John. "Public Speaking Anxiety and Fear of Brain Freezes." - National Social Anxiety Center. Feb. 20, 2017 https://nationalsocialanxietycenter.com/2017/02/20/public-speaking-and-fear-of-brain-freezes

failure on ineffective communication[41]. So even if you feel confident in your abilities, it never hurts to improve your communication skills.

I remember thinking that I was moments from death. No more than fourteen years old, I was invited to spend a warm summer day in a ski boat on the lake. An older teen drove the boat and I, somehow, had to be the first to put on skis. I had never water-skied before. None of us really knew what we were doing. As I bobbed in the water, awaiting my fate, the boat yanked suddenly. I tumbled and slammed to the surface, and found myself breathless, my diaphragm frozen, and I was unable to move. If not for the floatation device I wore, I would not have been able to keep my head above the water. In that moment, I was terrified. As the air returned to my lungs and the boat returned for me, I realized the folly in doing something dangerous with no instruction, preparation, or know-how.

It makes perfect sense to have at least a twinge of unsurety before speaking. If you are not prepared, trained, or coached and then told to put on skis, do your best, and try not to drown, there should be a sense of trepidation. So too, speaking without preparation, training, coaching, and a plan should scare anyone with common sense.

The next time I put on skis, I did not let the fear of past failure paralyze me. While still a little nervous, I listened carefully to instructions. I watched others who knew exactly what they were doing. I asked questions. I did not perform like a world-class water ski champion, but I did stay up on my skis long enough to completely enjoy the experience. If human brains have difficulty differentiating between a real physical threat and the unsurety of public speaking, then we should realize that the same attention to preparation can make a difference.

---

[41] Fierce, Inc. "2011 Survey: 85% of Employees Blame Lack of Collaboration or Ineffective Communication for Workplace Failures," May 4, 2011. https://fierceinc.com/employees-cite-lack-of-collaboration-for-workplace-failures.

BEFORE YOU START

Your masterful public address starts long before you take to the microphone. You may have weeks to prepare, or you may have just been tapped at the last minute to speak off the cuff. The preparation for presentation is still the same.

OUTLINE

Outlining your talk provides you with a roadmap of where you are verbally headed. If you lose your way, your outline will direct you back on course. Your first order of business is to determine your main point, your destination. Where do you want to take your audience?

Next, like making a travel itinerary, determine how you will lead your audience to that point. It makes no difference if you are giving a short thirty-second introduction or a long presentation. Just as if you were getting in your car and planning a trip to the grocery store or a cross-country trek, you still have to know your route.

Utilize the introduction, hook, story, lesson, ask, and out. Introduce yourself to connect with your audience. Hook them by meeting them where they are at and drawing them in with something they need. "This is what I'm going to do for you." Give a story, that human-interest portion that gives relatability and illustration to your point. Share your lesson, the meat or the main dish of the presentation. Give an ask that inspires your audience to action. Thank them for their time.

In that state convention, my speech was short and simple. See if you can identify the introduction, hook, story, lesson, ask, and out. "Ladies and gentlemen can I have your attention please?! I am Michelle Mendoza, and I am about to share with you a nomination that will inspire your hope in America! Once, on a Fourth of July, sitting by the bank of a river, I watched fireworks as a child. It was the very first time that the words of our national anthem came to life for me. I thought of the rockets' red glare and bombs bursting in air. I began to cry. I realized just how blessed I am to have the liberty that we all have as Americans and what price was paid for this freedom. If you understand that level of gratitude, then you can appreciate people like John, who earned a Purple Heart by risking his life to come between innocent civilians and an IED launched by terrorists. He continued the fight, as a man of color, supporting integration and understanding to mend differences in our communities. He still seeks to serve our nation, and you, today, as a delegate. Please join me in a round of applause of thanks and please give your support to John as a delegate to the national convention. Thank you."

NOTE IT

Notes, like crutches, can hold you up, steadying you as you verbally walk through your presentation. You cannot, however, run when using crutches. Notes work best when they are no more than bullet points. An over reliance on notes makes presentations less relatable and less sincere to your audience. The less time spent looking down at notes, the more engaging and effective your message.

The key is to keep it simple. While you may take time before your address to write out your speech, create PowerPoint slides, and research points but when it comes time to face the audience, less is more. Reading a speech at people is never as effective as speaking to people. Simplify your notes by reducing your research down to its outline and bullet points.

If you have six sections, introduction, hook, story, lesson, ask, and out, then your notes will have six segments. In my notes, I list numbers one through six with bullet points beneath each. My numbers and bullets are followed by one simple word, or a very short sentence to prompt me. This becomes my road map.

Jump in your car for a drive to a friend's place. You may turn on your map application for step-by-step directions. You can get a quick glance at a visual and hear the friendly voice say, "In one-hundred feet, turn left on to Second Street." This short and concise instruction gets you to where you need to go with minimal distraction. If the voice laid out extraneous instructions in paragraph form, you would likely miss your turn. Imagine it saying, "As you continue to drive you will, in about one-hundred feet, need to get into the left turn lane on the road you are driving on right now. You will need to turn left on to a street that is named Second Street." By the time all that was said, you would likely miss your turn. You get the picture. Think of your outline as your step-by-step directions to get you through your talk. Keep it simple and concise.

Subtle hand signals and the letters of the alphabet, in American sign language, are my chosen aid. With my left hand, I press my fingers to my thigh while making my way through the six segments of my talk, as though keeping count. My index finger is one, as I give my introduction. My middle finger, two, with my hook. The ring finger is three with the story. The lesson goes with my little finger, four. As I give the ask, my thumb is pressed to my side. With my other hand I remind myself of what comes next by forming the first letter of the next point. Then and only then if I really need to, I can look down at my notes for assistance.

EMOTIONALLY PREPARE

When water skiing or public speaking, we know that there is a level of risk involved, no matter what precautions one might take. Offset by preparation, the danger lessens. Yes, it is still there. Anxiety means you are human. Yet, emotionally preparing for any event can grant a little confidence and quell nerves. In that confidence the anxiety can turn into excitement.

Unlike the danger of drowning in a lake, giving a less than adequate performance on stage will not likely cost you your life. In fact, as we have discussed in prior chapters, your imperfections make you relatable to an audience. There is something inspirational in watching someone that is human and even fallible succeed in delivering an inspiring message right before our eyes. Success starts with a firm foundation of preparation.

Once you have your speech, your notes, your bullet points, and perspective, you have a foundation. Remembering that you possess a superpower and a super voice, use this opportunity as your moment to shine. Take a minute to bask in that surety and let it replace angst with enthusiasm.

BREATHE

Adrenalin takes over. Our air passages dilate, forcing oxygen away from our brain and into our body. Our muscles can shake and suddenly we are in fight or flight mode. In this condition, many have found the strength to survive and achieve superhuman feats. It can cause us to do things we would never think we were capable of.

"A nineteen-year-old teen named Charlotte Heffelmire not only lifted a burning truck off of her father, but she also saved her entire family from a possibly fatal fire. Her father Eric was working on his car in the garage when the jack slipped, pinning him, but that wasn't all. The impact of the car falling onto him caused gasoline to spill, which ignited all around the garage. Charlotte rushed into the garage and tried lifting the truck from her father. Charlotte said, "I lifted it the first time, he said 'OK, you almost got it,' finally managed to get it out, it was some crazy strength, and pulled him out." Examples of Charlotte's type of sudden weightlifting ability have also been coined as "hysterical strength".[42]

Adrenalin may grant temporary superhuman ability, but it also keeps you from thinking clearly. Who in their right mind would think that they could lift a burning truck off of a man? As you rise to the stage, adrenalin hits, with the side effect of muscles twitching and shaking from excess energy. Oxygen rushes to your body and unfortunately away from your brain. That makes it difficult to give a thought provoking or inspirational speech. That is why it is vital to "just breathe."

A few minutes before a public address, performance, appearance, or anything that causes a little anxiety, breathe. Pushing oxygen through your system, calming your nerves, and reoxygenating your brain will give you peace and focus. Concentrate on the points of your speech. You might also take your mind on a short vacation to somewhere peaceful. I start with a prayer.

EXERCISE

Try this exercise. Relax your tongue on the roof of your mouth. Breathe in through your nose for a five count. Make it a slow, even breath, aiming the air towards the bottom and back of your throat. Breathe that air deep into your diaphragm, as though you are filling your stomach with oxygen. Hold that

---

[42] Sara Pacella, "15 Times Adrenaline Took Over and Turned People Into Superhumans." The Richest. April 20, 2017. https://www.therichest.com/shocking/15-times-adrenaline-took-over-and-turned-people-into-superhumans/

breath for a five count. Exhale through your mouth with a hush sound for a count of five. Then sit still, counting to five, before starting the process again.

This amazing exercise pushes oxygen through your system and to your brain. It will quell nerves, anxiety, stress, and anger. It will still the anxiety and improve your focus.

AS YOU SPEAK

Now is the moment that you have been preparing for. You have found your foundation and inspiration. You have tapped into your niche and discovered your superpowers. You have trained yourself to shore up your weaknesses. You have found your voice and developed its message. You know exactly who you are addressing your message to. Now is your time to speak your voice to the waiting world. There are secrets that the best public speakers use to magnify their message's efficacy.

YOUR POSTURE

First impressions are everything. If you stand on the stage schlumped like a timid child, your audience will respond accordingly. Chin up, shoulders back, and a smile and look of confidence in your eyes will inspire confidence in what you are about to present.

As you stand before your audience take just a moment to connect. If you were to open the door to your home and welcome these folks in, what should your facial expression look like? Consider this part of your introduction. Take this moment to look over the crowd, your host, or the camera, and smile as though you are looking directly at your listener avatar. Take in one more deep breath and begin.

EYE CONTACT

Just as looking down at notes repels an audience, eye contact connects. Yet, it is a tricky thing. If you have been in a crowd and a speaker makes prolonged eye contact with you, it can make you feel uncomfortable. Brief contact connects without discomfort. One way to give the appearance of connection is to look just over the heads of your audience, changing your focal point every few seconds or so. If you need to look down at your notes, try to not break the mood by maintaining a consistent facial expression.

Believe it or not, eye contact is just as important for audio. When broadcasting, I either have an image of my ideal listener framed in my studio, or I image them in my head as I speak. Talking to someone specific, rather than at someone creates sincere engagement.

SPEAK TO THE BACK OF THE ROOM

The last person in the last row is as important as the guy sitting directly in front of you. While yelling will not endear you to anyone, a strong, sure voice will invoke a sense of self-assurance. Even if you are aided by a sound system and microphones, your communication to the person in the back makes the entire room feel included.

SLOW DOWN

It is quite natural, as you stand before peering eyes or in a broadcast, to speak at a faster pace. Your voice will rise in pitch and your breathing will become shallow. Sometimes voices become shrill and off-putting. From your very first word, purposefully try to speak low and slow. Slowing your roll gives you more control. It aids in enunciation, so that your words are clear and crisp. It gives your listener a better chance at really getting your message. The slow down method will transform your speaking power and give your words more weight.

PURPOSEFUL PAUSING

Silence may sometimes be golden. Pausing for effect allows your listener to catch up, to ponder, and to feel the points of your message. As does repeating an important phrase or portion of your message. In the times that you lose your focus or find yourself grasping for your next point, do yourself a favor. Do not *break character*. Pause with purpose.

Breaking character is a theatrical term describing what takes place when an actor, in a performance, is playing a character then suddenly stops acting as their character would. This can break engagement with the viewer. In a speaking engagement, do not break the moment by breaking character. Use the moment to stand in confidence, smile assuredly, and pause. You might repeat your last statement, which can often get you back on track. Find your place in your notes. Then begin speaking again all without breaking character or changing your expression.

SMILE

If you do lose your way, if you feel the twinge of nerves coming upon you, breath and smile. Take a moment to give an honest, genuine, "I care", smile. A smile relieves stress and tricks your body into elevating its mood. Smiling helps your audience to relax and feel at ease. It endears you to them and gives a feeling of well-being to all. When all is said and your words are done, finish your talk with a grateful smile.

Practice makes perfect. Before a mirror or in front of trusted friends, practice the tools of the communication trade. Like getting up on skis, the first time might be shaky, but it need not be miserable. As you participate in the sport of speaking, you will improve with each opportunity.

There is nary a human being that can escape the platform of public communication. From job interviews, business connections, customer service interactions, to taking marriage vows before friends and family, communication is at the heart of our involvement in society.

The thirty-eighth president of the United States, Gerald R. Ford once said, "You can speak well if your tongue can deliver the message of your heart." If all else fails, remember that at the heart of your words is your passion. It is your voice.

SECTION 5

CELEBRATE YOUR VOICE

*The more you praise and celebrate your life,
the more there is in life to celebrate.*

—Oprah Winfrey, American actress and talk-show host

CHAPTER 19:

CELEBRATE YOUR VOICE

THE WONDER OF Christmas, as a child, can be an enchanting. I can recall the last fading hours of Christmas eve. The house was hushed; the hustle and bustle finally ceased. The darkness of the winter was illuminated softly by the warm lights that reflected their glow off of bobbles on the Christmas tree. Brightly wrapped boxes lay still as they sleepily guarded the mystery treasures held within. My mother loved Christmas and gladly went into debt each year to fill our humble living room with seemingly endless gifts. Come Christmas day, it was hard to navigate a passage through the boxes, as presents piled upon presents seemed to multiply.

Excitement made for a long, restless sleep. Waking up too early, I would watch the clock, counting the seconds in the minutes and minutes in the hour until it was time. When morning finally broke, I would race to the tree. The explosion of paper, boxes, and ribbon revealed their objects of fascination. Oh, how I can recall the magic!

Strangely, looking back, I remember few of the actual gifts. What I do remember is the look of joy on my mother's face as we burst with excitement. I hear the songs we sung and the feeling of comfort that comes from being surrounded by family. I remember sitting on the carpet playing with my new gifts with my father, his eyes tired from late night toy assembly. I can almost breathe in the smell of dinner cooking as my mom sung carols in her off-tune voice. I close my eyes and these memories flood my soul and comfort me. I may have missed this truth as a child but today I understand that there is so much more to the gift of Christmas.

As I harken back to children's television memories, I recall one of Mister Roger's phrases that reminds me of what the best gift we can ever give is, at Christmas or at any other occasion. He said that "The greatest gift you ever give is your honest self." This is a prize of invaluable worth. It is what gave real meaning to my holiday celebration and what will give your voice power.

If I could encapsulate in a phrase the wealth of my experience and knowledge in communications and all of the efforts of this book, it would come down to the simple realization that the greatest gift you ever give is your honest self. Thanks, Mister Rogers!

Dig deep to connect with your real honest self. Give it voice. That voice expressed is your gift to the world. You can wrap it in whatever platform you choose. You can perfect it upon each presentation. It can be boisterously shouted or softly spoken. However you present it, it is a priceless gift you can give to those with whom you share it.

As glorious as Christmas has always been to me, there was the days after when the tree was taken down, the decorations put away, and the excitement ceased. Seasons change in the cycle of sharing our voice. Enthusiasm will rise and wane. Those who feed their souls, by celebrating their honest self in gratitude, will find reasons to celebrate in every season of life.

You are a masterpiece in progress. Every day and each new experience paint another brush stroke on your work. Some are displayed in bright happy tones and others in dark harsh strokes. They all work together to complete the story of your life, a story that someone else's life will be enhanced by hearing.

Earlier I shared a scientific theory that it may take all of the elements of the entire universe to support life on Earth, the anthropic principle. If this is true, think of the implications. Everything works together to make this gift of life continue. You are more important than any rock, star, planet, plant, or animal. You are God's workmanship. You were made in this time in history to hold a vital role. The talents, personality, communications superpowers, and life experiences that you were blessed with become part of your gift. All of the elements that make you work together to form your voice. That voice is an essential part of the universe. It is a melody that is part of your magnum opus, a song that will surely become all the more beautiful the more it is sung.

Can you recall the enthusiasm in celebrating Christmas, Chanukah, or your birthday, as a child? Have you ever felt the rumbling thrill of the crowd as your team fought against the odds to win a game? Has there ever been a time that you tossed your head back and threw your hands into the air in celebration? With that kind of passion, I ask that you daily celebrate you and the One who made you. Walk in gratitude, joy, and hope. Purpose to use your voice to touch lives in even the smallest way, as only you can. Never, ever, let your voice be silenced. After all, you were born for such a time as this.

I have delighted in sharing my voice and my journey with you, dear reader. It is born from my honest self, and it is my gift to you. My hope is that your own beautiful, unique, and irreplaceable voice will exhibit like a magnum opus, a gift to the world. Speak it out in confidence and joy and never, ever cease!

www.ingramcontent.com/pod-product-compliance
Lightning Source LLC
LaVergne TN
LVHW041320080426
835513LV00008B/526

9 781940 025698